John E. Riley Library
Northwest Nazarene University
Nampa, Idaho

P9-BHS-724

ALTERNATE
ASSESSMENTS
for STUDENTS
With DISABILITIES

DATE DUE

LC
4031
.A62
2001

ALTERNATE ASSESSMENTS for STUDENTS With DISABILITIES

Sandra J. Thompson
Rachel F. Quenemoen
Martha L. Thurlow
James E. Ysseldyke

A joint publication of the
Council for Exceptional Children
and Corwin Press, Inc.

Council for
Exceptional
Children

CORWIN PRESS, INC.
A Sage Publications Company
Thousand Oaks, California

Copyright ©2001 by Corwin Press, Inc.

All rights reserved. When forms and sample documents are included, their use is authorized only by educators, local school sites, and/or noncommercial entities who have purchased the book. Except for that usage, no part of this book may be reproduced or utilized in any form or by any means, electronic or mechanical, including photocopying, recording, or by any information storage and retrieval system, without permission in writing from the publisher.

For information:

Corwin Press, Inc.
A Sage Publications Company
2455 Teller Road
Thousand Oaks, California 91320
E-mail: order@corwinpress.com

Sage Publications Ltd.
6 Bonhill Street
London EC2A 4PU
United Kingdom

Sage Publications India Pvt. Ltd.
M-32 Market
Greater Kailash I
New Delhi 110 048 India

Printed in the United States of America

Library of Congress Cataloging-in-Publication Data

Main entry under title:

Alternate assessments for students with disabilities / by Sandra J.
    Thompson ... [et al.].
        p.   cm.
    Includes bibliographical references and index.
    ISBN 0-7619-7773-2 (cloth: alk. paper)
    ISBN 0-7619-7774-0 (pbk.: alk. paper)
    1. Handicapped children—Education—United States.   2. Handicapped
students—Rating of—United States.   3. Educational tests and
measurements—United States.   I. Thompson, Sandra J.
    LC4031.A62   2001
    371.9′0973—dc21   2001000297

This book is printed on acid-free paper.

01 02 03 04 05 06 07   7 6 5 4 3 2 1

Acquiring Editor:	Robb Clouse
Corwin Editorial Assistant:	Kylee Liegl
Production Editor:	Diane S. Foster
Editorial Assistant:	Candice Crosetti
Typesetter/Designer:	Janelle LeMaster
Cover Designer:	Michael Dubowe

Table of Contents

CORWIN
PRESS

The Corwin Press logo—a raven striding across an open book—represents the happy union of courage and learning. We are a professional-level publisher of books and journals for K–12 educators, and we are committed to creating and providing resources that embody these qualities. Corwin's motto is "Success for All Learners."

Preface

In writing this book, we thought long and hard about the best ways to make alternate assessment real, to make it come alive for readers. We had lots of information and data, including federal and state laws, requirements, and guidelines and state status reports, but we knew that it would take much more to convince people of the importance of alternate assessments. We also knew about the "blood, sweat, and tears" shed by people who advocated for alternate assessment to become law. We knew they had committed to that struggle on behalf of specific young people in their own lives who attended school but who didn't really count in efforts to improve schooling through standards-based reform.

We realized that we needed the stories of these young people. We needed to talk about real students who had participated, at least in pilot tests, in actual alternate assessments in real states. We also realized that we couldn't make up those stories—when we said "real" we had to mean it. With that in mind, we would like to present a young student we'll call Lara (not her real name), an 8th grader who participated in her state's first challenging year of alternate assessment implementation. Lara will appear in every chapter of this book, along with the stories of other children—including our own. Thanks to them and their stories, the purpose and use of alternate assessment has come alive for us as we hope it will for you.

MEET LARA ❖

Lara is a 14-year-old 8th grader attending a small-town junior high school. She lives with her parents and grandmother. Lara has multiple disabilities, including cerebral palsy and severe mental retardation. She has had surgery several times to maintain some range of motion and strength. She receives nourishment through a gastrointestinal tube at night and continues to work on eating (chewing and swallowing) during the day. When she gets to school, if it is cold outside, Lara needs to be warmed up, and if it is warm outside, she needs to be cooled off because her body temperature doesn't regulate itself. This is often done by changing her clothes before she can be situated for the day.

At lunchtime, Lara is working on swallowing about an ounce of fluid. She begins by using a chew bag to stimulate her chewing reflexes and get her juices started, and then, about 45 minutes later, she is ready to swallow. Lara has daily occupational and physical therapy, along with extensive care of her physical needs, including diaper changing. Lara has had little voluntary involvement in any of these activities.

Lara's levels of vision and hearing are hard to determine, and she vocalizes by yelling or crying. Lara uses a wheelchair, and all of her personal care needs are taken care of by others. Her cognitive ability has not been measurable through any standardized means, so she has never been tested.

Even though Lara attends a regular public school, she comes to school on a special bus, at a different time from the other students, and in the past, spent the entire day with an educational assistant in a special education resource room. Lara was fed in the classroom and taken for a walk around the school building in the afternoon but had no contact with any peers.

Last year, Lara's school volunteered to participate in a pilot implementation of her state's new alternate assessment system. Over that year, her Individualized Education Program (IEP) team learned that she could indeed learn—that she can make choices and work toward the high standards set for all students across her state. Through each chapter of this book, we will follow Lara's progress and watch how alternate assessment challenged beliefs about what Lara can learn and how Lara's goals and activities in her daily life—at school, at home, and in the community—have been changed. We will tell the story of how Lara's life has been transformed by high expectations, by careful assessment of her progress, and by her school's accountability for her learning.

Change Is Tough

Change is tough, and the move to high expectations, assessments, and accountability for student learning is a big change for many people. What does it take for people to try something new, to make a difficult change? We understand that change does not happen until people reach a threshold in their dissatisfaction with the way things are—in other words, they see a need based on their own perceptions of and concerns for what is important. Through this book, we hope to raise your level of concern about a group of students who have been unimportant in many schools in the past—students like Lara, students who deserve not only access to schools but access to high-quality schooling. We hope to significantly raise your concern for students with significant disabilities so that you will be willing to commit to change and not accept "exemption" as an option within schools any longer. We want the phrase "all students can learn" to be at the top of every school's list of beliefs or principles, and we want "all means *all*" to be clearly understood. Alternate assessments, as we hope to make clear on every page of this book, have the potential to operationalize this message, making "all students can learn" a measurable reality.

We understand how long it takes to establish such a difficult and complex change. We have studied research on the process of change within educational systems, and we know that we have embarked on a long, complex, and difficult journey. We know that a single workshop, conference session, lecture, or even book will not result in substantial change, but each can serve as a catalyst to move all of us in the direction of inclusive educational systems, measured by inclusive assessments.

In Lara's case, the learning curve for her parents and other IEP team members was very steep—from acceptance of complacent day care for Lara to high expectations for Lara's learning. Lara's school staff, as well as her IEP team, had to learn about standards and how to assess her performance toward them because, for the first time, they were accountable for her learning via the alternate assessments, not just for her care. For other teams, in schools where expectations and support have already been very high, the change will be a matter of minimal adjustment in what they teach and how they assess student progress toward standards. We expect that most IEP teams and schools will fall somewhere in between the two extremes.

Something to Think About

We believe this book will help teams move forward, but a few cautions are in order. We will show you how to shift to high expectations for all learners, how to carefully assess their progress, and how to use the assessment data you gather to improve schooling for them. We will do so based on the experience of states and districts across the country. But what we describe is evolving as we write. Standards-based instruction, assessment, and accountability are new for all schools and students, and in most states and districts, we're learning how best to do this as we go. We're describing a "moving target" in this book. Thus, although we give many, many examples of district and state practice, we have elected in most cases to not identify state or district names. We think this approach will avoid confusion that might occur if a state practice has changed by the time you read the book. Still, we are giving you many concrete examples with which to build your understanding of alternate assessment.

We offer you a big picture of high expectations, assessment, and accountability for students with significant disabilities. We will guide you through the process of alternate assessment from beginning to end, based on our understanding of and beliefs about best practices as they stand right now. Several chapters include examples of worksheets and forms that have worked for some teachers and in some settings and our best insights into how they can be used to help your students. But policies and practices in your state or district may be somewhat different from what we present. You'll need to look at what your state and district require; we offer suggestions on how to do that throughout the book. Make the ideas from this book your own, in a way that meets your needs in your particular setting. This book can empower you to better understand your own state or district requirements and to get the most out of whatever alternate assessment approach you use.

Last, we hope that you can tap into the staff development resources that your state and district offer. Most states have training resources available, and most states build their training on best-practice models in staff development. This book can serve as a resource for planning staff development from the state or district level, or the information can be used by collegial "learning communities" within schools. We encourage you to take these materials and build on them through professional networking. By the time the next edition of this book is released, we know that it is our readers, those of you who work with and support these children, who will have taught us the newest and best practices to ensure that all children learn! We look forward to learning from you.

▪ AUDIENCE

We wrote this book as a resource for both general and special educators at all grade levels, parents of students with disabilities at all ages, advocates, education policy leaders, and others concerned about the inclusion of all students in educational reform efforts. In addition, the primary audience for this book includes professionals responsible for development, training, implementation, and continuous improvement of alternate assessments at the state and local levels. This includes state agency specialists and consultants, school district administrators and coordinators, university faculty and instructors, and undergraduate and graduate students. Because the primary participants in alternate assessments are students with significant disabilities, professional associations targeting services for these students will also be particularly interested in the content of this book.

▪ ACKNOWLEDGMENTS

We would like to acknowledge the careful and thoughtful work of state and local educators and administrators in the states of Arkansas and Wyoming who worked with us on the design of the alternate assessment processes described in this book.

We extend special thanks to Patti Whetstone, an educational diagnostic consultant and former Wyoming director of special education, for providing us with stories about real students—the students for whom this book was written.

About the Authors

The authors of this book represent diverse views and experiences, from intensive practice to extensive research to legislative and policy skills; with special and general education experiences in classroom, building, district, state, national, and university arenas; and in the roles of teachers, parent of a person with a disability, researchers, state and cooperative administrators, and advocates. Collectively, the authors offer demonstrated experience and resources in many areas critical to the development of this book. Among these critical areas are the following:

- A national perspective on the participation of students with disabilities in national, state, and local assessment systems, including the articulation of standards, assessment accommodations, and alternate assessments that will ensure full participation

- Experience in documenting state and local assessment systems, including specification of standards, participation, and accommodation guidelines and alternate assessment development

- Technical expertise and experience in the development of large-scale assessment systems, including an understanding of technical issues associated with alternate assessments

- Direct linkage to states, including chief state school officers, assessment directors, and special education directors, as well as connections to districts through state organizations

- Direct linkage to other national, state, and local groups concerned with educational reform, particularly as it relates to the Individuals with Disabilities Education Act (IDEA) and Title I, Improving America's Schools Act

- Standing within both general and special education communities that facilitates research, collaboration, and the provision of technical assistance

- A proven track record in designing and operating a system of technical assistance to districts and states

Rachel F. Quenemoen, MS, is the National Center on Educational Outcome's (NCEO) Technical Assistance and Dissemination Area Leader. She has 25 years of experience as an educational sociologist and as a parent of a young person with a disability. She specializes in "research into practice" efforts aimed at building the capacity of the end users of information. She has planned and implemented local, state, and national change processes for major school reform efforts. Working with graduation standards at an individual school level, she worked on pilot development of graduation standards and project-based learning aligned to standards for *all* students. For a 90-district collaborative, she developed and implemented early-childhood, low-incidence, and technology-assisted special education programs, interagency services, and later, collaborative services. For a state, she worked with transition from school to adult life (a State Systems Change grant), a state school-to-work initiative, and developing a state's accountability system.

As a researcher, she has done national survey research in educational technology and intensive qualitative field research on the social construction of the "least restrictive environment" at the school and classroom levels. Her current research focus includes gray areas of assessment systems, best practices in state and district policies and procedures, social promotion, Title I assessment and school improvement linkages, content-performance standards issues for inclusive accountability systems, and the design and implementation of alternate assessment systems. She has published, presented, and trained on topics related to large-scale assessment, planning, content and performance standards, transition, and school-to-work for policymakers, professionals, parents, and students.

Sandra J. Thompson, PhD, serves as a research associate at NCEO at the University of Minnesota where she has been responsible for state survey research activities that document the status of outcomes for students with disabilities, current assessment policies and practices, and involvement with *IDEA* activities.

She has an extensive background in preparing students with disabilities for successful adult lives. Prior to joining NCEO, she spent nearly 10 years with Minnesota's department of education as a special education administrator focusing on educational experiences and outcomes for students with disabilities. She also spent 10 years as a special education teacher, working with students with developmental disabilities. She has coordinated multiple research activities, including online surveys addressing the development of alternate assessments across states and the inclusion of students with disabilities in state accountability systems. She has assisted several states in the design of inclusive assessment systems, developing tools for determining inclusive assessment practices. She has published a number of newsletters, journal articles, technical reports, and training manuals. She has facilitated numerous district, state, and national training events.

Martha L. Thurlow, PhD, is the director of NCEO at the University of Minnesota. She has 30 years of research experience, with a strong emphasis on policy-related issues in special education. Over the years, she has served as research coordinator and study site liaison on numerous major research projects, including those focusing on the assessment and decision-making process for students with learning disabilities and children in early-childhood special education programs; postschool outcomes for students with mild, moderate, or severe mental retardation and other disabilities; evaluation of students with disabilities in the mainstream; dropout prevention and intervention; and assessment of social outcomes and networks of individuals with mild, moderate, and severe mental retardation and learning disabilities. She also has directed a leadership training effort.

Dr. Thurlow was a member of the National Research Council (NRC) committee that produced *Educating One & All: Standards-Based Reform and Students with Disabilities,* and also has spoken to other NRC committees. She has presented on the participation of students with disabilities in national and state reforms, to the National Education Goals Panel, the National Assessment Governing Board, which oversees the national assessment of educational progress, and numerous other groups concerned with educational reform and students with disabilities.

She has expertise and experience in information dissemination through her coordination of large-scale dissemination activities in institutes devoted to research on children with disabilities, including the Institute for Research on Learning Disabilities and the Institute on Community Integration (University Affiliated Program). She has organized the writing of research-to-practice publications, conducted major working conferences, and coordinated national dissemination strategies.

She has published several book chapters, more than 80 refereed journal articles, 150 technical reports, and numerous other requested materials. She is an author of three major books: *Critical Issues in Special Education, Testing Students with Disabilities: Practical Strategies for Complying with District and State Requirements,* and *Improving the Test Performance of Students with Disabilities.* She currently is coeditor of *Exceptional Children,* the research journal of the Council for Exceptional Children.

James E. Ysseldyke, PhD, is Birkmaier Professor of Educational Leadership and Associate Dean for Research at the University of Minnesota. He is a recognized leader in the areas of assessment and special-remedial education. Previously, he was Director of NCEO, Director of the Minnesota Institute for Research on Learning Disabilities, and Director of the National School Psychology Inservice Training Network.

His research and writing have focused on issues in assessing and making instructional decisions about students with disabilities. He has authored over 20 books. His most recent are *Special Education: A Practical Approach for Teachers, Assessment, Critical Issues in Special Education* and *The Challenge of Complex School Problems.* He has published an instructional environment system (TIES-2) and an effective-instruction program (Strategies and Tactics for Effective Instruction). He has served as editor of eight professional journals. He has been an invited speaker and presenter at international, national, and state conferences. He has served as an adviser to the Early Childhood Longitudinal Study and the Office of Educational Research and Improvement's National Institute on Student Achievement, Curriculum, and Assessment.

Over the years, Dr. Ysseldyke has received more than 20 awards for his scholarly accomplishments. Honors include being the first recipient of the Lightner Witmer Award presented by the School Psychology Division of the American Psychological Association, the distinguished teaching award presented by the University of Minnesota, and the Guest of Honor of the American Educational Research Association. He was the 1995 recipient of the Council for Exceptional Children Research Award.

1

Alternate Assessment

What and Why

TOUGH QUESTIONS

Why should standards-based reform affect students who receive special education services, since their education plan is already individualized and tailored to their unique learning needs?

I understand why we need to measure student progress toward standards, and I expect schools to help all students be successful. But students with the most severe disabilities can't really learn anything other than some really basic functional skills anyway, can they?

What difference does it make whether we're measuring students with the most severe disabilities? There really are not many of them, and the gains they make are almost immeasurable.

- All children can learn.
- All children thrive in an atmosphere of high expectations about what they will learn.
- If all children are expected to learn and they have had opportunities to reach high expectations, all children can be successful.

Do you agree with these statements?

Think about the children you know. Do those statements fit Troy, the high-achieving student who just won the state spelling bee? What about Callie, who raised her grades from all Cs to mostly As after getting support for a learning disability? And do they apply to Lara, whom you met in the Preface, an 8th grader who is nonverbal, requires extensive physical care, and has never left the special education resource room? Do those statements fit Tony and Becca, the students described here?

Tony ▬

Tony is a 12-year-old student in 6th grade. Tony uses a wheelchair but is able to walk with a walker for short periods of time. He is able to feed himself, but someone needs to prepare the food by chopping it into small pieces and then monitoring him while he eats. Tony has been diagnosed with visual and hearing loss and wears hearing aids and glasses. He is typically cooperative when working hand-over-hand with any task but needs signals to continue the job on his own. Tony has no coherent verbal language but does make vocalizations. Tony is able to sign "more" when he is eating. We are working on signing "more food." It is difficult to determine whether or not the vocalizations signify pleasure or displeasure. Tony does not seem to indicate discomfort. He does, however, reach over his chair to put on his jacket at times during the day. Whether it is because he is cold or for comfort is unknown. Tony's cognitive skills, at this point, have not been measurable.

Becca ▬

Becca is a 9-year-old 4th grader with Down syndrome. She attends general education classes most of the day with accommodations and special education support. She is able to decode words at about a 2nd-grade level but does not always understand what she reads. Writing is slow and laborious, due both to difficulty holding a pencil and difficulty remembering how to spell many words. Becca speaks in two- to three-word sentences and follows two-step directions. She can count and do simple math computation. She is learning to use a calculator so she can buy things.

Do you think Tony and Becca can learn? Should we have high expectations for their learning? Can they be successful? The answers we each give to these questions have a lot to do with the challenges and opportunities of alternate assessment. A brief review of the recent push for standards-based reform helps us understand why.

❋ A BIT OF EDUCATIONAL HISTORY

For many years, schools were based on the premise that many students can learn the content and skills typically offered in schools to an acceptable level of competence, some students can learn at very high levels, and some students really can't learn much at all. In the past, schooling as a social system helped sort out which students were which, helped select which students would go on to college, which would go on to trades, and which would do manual labor or need to be institutionalized. We used the same curriculum and instructional methods for most students, and we measured students with standardized, norm-referenced tests that allowed us to determine where each student was in the "normal" distribution of learning. We became comfortable with the bell-shaped curve with many students in the middle and a few students at either end of assessment results. We saw strong correlations between socioeconomic status and achievement, and we assumed that these correlations simply demonstrated a tendency for successful parents to have successful children. We assumed that this simply reflected reality.

That premise was challenged by the end of the 1980s, when business and political leaders realized that the changing economy required many more workers who could do very high levels of work. If the economy was to grow, more of our students had to be more successful at learning, from basic skills to very high levels of critical thinking. At the same time, research on teaching and learning was leading us to question our premise that not all children can learn. Among practitioners, new emphasis was placed on effective schooling practices in instruction and curriculum. Among policymakers, new emphasis was placed, first, on defining what skills would be required of the workforce in the 21st century and then, on determining how to retool schooling to get all students to those skill levels. From the combination of political and economic need, along with research-driven educational-practice concerns, the standards-based reform movement was born.

The premise of standards-based reform is very different from the previous premise of a bell-shaped curve for student performance. The premise is that all students can be expected to learn, although some may need more time and varied instruction, and that these high expectations can be operationalized by articulating what all students must know and be able to do and to what levels. The challenge facing us is to provide opportunities for all students to learn and to hold schools accountable for their learning.

That brings us back to the opening statements:

- All children can learn.
- All children thrive in an atmosphere of high expectations about what they will learn.
- If all children are expected to learn and they have had opportunities to reach high expectations, all children can be successful.

And it brings us to a focus on the specifics of standards-based reform and how students like Lara, Tony, and Becca fit into the word "all."

OVERVIEW OF STANDARDS-BASED REFORM ✖

In the past decade, several federal laws have helped reshape our approach to ensuring that all students succeed. Although these may not seem to be relevant to our discussion about alternate assessments, they are. In 1994, Congress reauthorized the Elementary and Secondary Education Act (ESEA), and within the Title I provisions of the Act, shifted the focus of compensatory education. This reauthorization, called the Improving America's Schools Act (IASA) of 1994, required that in Title I–funded schools we must expect that the disadvantaged children served by Title I will meet the same challenging standards for student achievement we expect of other children (see Box 1.1).

Box 1.1

— *Guidance on Standards, Assessments, and Accountability That Supplements the Elementary & Secondary Education Act as Amended by the Improving America's Schools Act of 1994, P.L. 103-382 (1997)*

"The emphasis on challenging content and student performance standards for all children provides a clear goal for the new Title I law: to enable children served by Title I to meet the challenging standards established by the State for all its children. States, districts, and schools are called on to break with past practice by replacing minimum standards for some children with challenging standards for all. . . . States that have developed content and performance standards that apply to all children must also use them for Title I purposes." (I. Content and Performance Standards, Introduction, p. 1 of 8)

To measure how well children served by Title I are doing, we have to measure student progress toward those standards through an assessment system aligned to the standards. Furthermore, *all* students in the school are held to these standards, and the progress of *all* students is measured by these assessments and reported to the public. Based on the assessment reports, schools will make the instructional and structural changes needed so that the expectations of all students are raised as they have opportunities to work toward high standards (see Box 1.2).

Students with disabilities are specifically included in the definition of "all" in IASA 1994, and the amendments to the Individuals with Disabilities Education Act of 1997 (IDEA 97) further clarify Congressional expectations. IDEA 1997 focuses state and district attention on the challenges of full participation of students with disabilities in assessment systems and on the challenges of understanding and developing inclusive accountability systems that will improve outcomes for all students. These laws were designed from the results of 20 years of research, demonstration, and practice that have suggested that in schools where all students are expected to succeed, all students do succeed (see Box 1.3).

Think about our opening statements:

- All children can learn.
- All children thrive in an atmosphere of high expectations about what they will learn.
- If all children are expected to learn, and they have had opportunities to reach high expectations, all children can be successful.

These statements reflect the national commitment to all students through standards-based reform, as defined in IASA 1994 and IDEA 1997.

For the past 25 years, since the passage of P.L. 94-142, those of us in special education have tended to understand the requirements and purposes of special education to be somehow separate from general education. We focused on the individual needs of the students we served as was required, but sometimes we overlooked the importance of our services in helping the students succeed in the general curriculum. Almost as a reminder to us, IDEA 1997 clearly builds on the requirements of IASA 1994 and specifically requires that all students have access to the general curriculum and, to the extent

Box 1.2

— *Elementary & Secondary Education Act as Amended by the Improving America's Schools Act of 1994, P.L. 103-382 (1994)*

"Such assessments shall . . . provide for—the reasonable adaptations and accommodations for students with diverse learning needs, necessary to measure the achievement of such students relative to State content standards." (Sec. 1111 (b)(3)(F)(ii))

"Each State plan shall demonstrate that the State has developed or adopted a set of high-quality, yearly student assessments . . . that will be used as the primary means of determining the yearly performance of each local educational agency and schools served under this part in enabling all children served under this part to meet the State's student performance standards. Such assessments shall—(A) be the same assessments used to measure the performance of all children, if the State measures the performance of all children; (B) be aligned with the State's challenging content and student performance standards and provide coherent information about student attainment of such standards; (C) be used for purposes for which such assessments are valid and reliable, and be consistent with relevant, nationally recognized professional and technical standards for such assessments; (D) measure the proficiency of students in the academic subjects in which a State has adopted challenging content and student performance standards and be administered at some time during—(i) grades 3 through 5; (ii) grades 6 through 9; and (iii) grades 10 through 12; (E) involve multiple up-to-date measures of student performance, including measures that assess higher order thinking skills and understanding; (F) provide for—the participation in such assessments of all students . . . ; (G) include students who have attended schools in a local educational agency for a full academic year but have not attended a single school for a full academic year, however the performance of students who have attended more than one school in the local educational agency in any academic year shall be used only in determining the progress of the local educational agency." (Sec. 1111 (b)(3))

— *Guidance on Standards, Assessments, and Accountability That Supplements the Elementary & Secondary Education Act as Amended by the Improving America's Schools Act of 1994, P.L. 103-382 (1997)*

"Assessments for Title I purposes focus on whether the yearly performance of each LEA and school served under Title I is enabling all children served to meet the State's student performance standards. It is important that students with disabilities be included in these assessments because they are expected to meet the same standards as other students." (II. Assessments, Question #42, p. 10 of 16)

appropriate, be working toward the same high standards. We still must weigh carefully the needs of the individual student in designing services that support that student's progress toward standards, but we are reminded that *all* students must be expected to work toward high standards.

But does "all" really include Lara? Or Tony? Or Becca? In Chapter 2, we take a closer look at how these standards apply to students like Lara, Tony, and Becca and how an IEP team can determine how each student can progress toward high standards. We also address what it may mean for students like Lara, Becca, and Tony to be "successful" in their work toward standards.

Box 1.3

▬ *Amendments to the Individuals with Disabilities Education Act, P.L. 105-17 (1997)*

"Such research, demonstrations, and practice over the past 20 years in special education and related disciplines have demonstrated that an effective educational system now and in the future must maintain high academic standards and clear performance goals for children with disabilities, consistent with the standards and expectations for all students in the educational system, and provide for appropriate and effective strategies and methods to ensure that students who are children with disabilities have maximum opportunities to achieve those standards and goals." (Section 651(a)(6)(A))

Box 1.4

▬ *Final Regulations for the Amendments to the Individuals with Disabilities Education Act, P.L. 105-17 (1999)*

"The new law has a goal of including children with disabilities in the general curriculum and improving results for these children, in contrast to the focus in prior law of simply providing disabled children access to public schools." (General comments, p.12537)

In summary, standards-based reform includes these assumptions:

- *All* children are expected to work toward state or district high standards.
- States and districts measure *all* children's progress toward the standards.
- Schools use measurement data to make improvements in curriculum and instruction to allow *all* children to succeed.
- States, districts, and schools are held accountable for student success.

And the laws make it clear that *all* children means **all** children. IDEA 1997 specifically defines the shift in thinking from earlier laws (see Box 1.4).

In addition to Title I and special education federal laws specifying that all children are to be working toward high standards, the Office of Civil Rights also reinforces the national commitment to equal opportunity for all students and defines that equity of opportunity as a student right (see Box 1.5).

✛ STATE LAWS AND IMPLEMENTATION

Many states have built on this national commitment with state legislation, rules, and guidelines that further define the nature of standards-based reform in the state. To make the best use of the information in this book, it is important for you to gather information from your school, district, or state administrators to ensure that you address the requirements of both federal and state law and any local requirements that may exist.

Box 1.5

— *The Use of Tests When Making High-Stakes Decisions for Students: A Resource Guide for Educators and Policymakers, U.S. Dept. of Education, Office of Civil Rights (July 6, 2000 Draft)*

"Importantly, tests can help indicate inequalities in the kinds of educational opportunities students are receiving, and in turn, they may stimulate efforts to ensure that all students have equal opportunity to achieve high standards." And on p. 16 of the report, "Providing effective instruction in the general education curriculum for students with disabilities is an important aspect of providing a free appropriate public education." (p. iv, Letter from the Assistant Secretary)

It is important to understand your state's approach thoroughly to be able to effectively involve the students you serve in this reform. Almost all state Web sites provide comprehensive information about the state's approach to school reform. The Council of Chief State School Officers (CCSSO) maintains a Web page that links to every state's education Web site with a click of the mouse. That Web page is at http://www.ccsso.org/seamenu.html.

ACCOUNTABILITY, ASSESSMENT, ✖ AND TESTING DEFINED

So far, we've used the terms *accountability* and *assessment* as important parts of standards-based reform. Understanding the differences between these terms and the related term, *testing,* is important in understanding how *all* children can be successful. Under Federal law, *all* students are expected to work toward the same high expectations or standards. States and districts must measure how well students are doing by using assessments that are aligned to standards. One common method of assessment is tests, sometimes called *large-scale assessments* when used for accountability purposes. Based on assessment results, school improvement teams work to improve curriculum and instruction so that all children can succeed. States, districts, and schools are accountable for the results of all children, and looking at the assessment results tell us whether schools are moving in the direction of success for all children.

So, what do these terms mean?

- *Accountability* is a process to report and analyze student results in all schools and districts to ensure that the public and educators can identify and address needed improvements. The Education Commission of the States (ECS) defines accountability as a "systematic collection, analysis, and use of information to hold schools, educators, and others responsible for the performance of students and the education system" (ECS, 1999).
- *Assessment* is the use of data to make decisions and in the context of this book, specifically to make decisions about improving schools or student progress (Salvia & Ysseldyke, 2001).
- *Testing* is one way to gather assessment information, typically resulting in a student or group score (Salvia & Ysseldyke, 2001).

Box 1.6

— *Final Regulations for the Amendments to the Individuals with Disabilities Education Act, P.L. 105-17 (1997)*

"The IDEA Amendments of 1997 require that all children with disabilities be included in general State and districtwide assessment programs, with appropriate accommodations, where necessary. In some cases, alternate assessments may be necessary, depending on the needs of the child, and not the category or severity of the child's disability." (Content of IEP, Discussion, pp. 12593-12594)

✖ ASSESSMENT AND ACCOUNTABILITY SYSTEMS

If we improve our schools by measuring the progress of our students, then who should be measured? To ensure that all students have opportunities to learn to high standards, *all* students must be measured. Not all students are assessed exactly the same way, but *all* students fit into a system of assessment aligned to a set of standards. Yet individual students sometimes require particular approaches to assessment to show what they know and are able to do. For example, a student who is blind cannot read and respond to a pencil-and-paper test, even if the student knows and understands the content on the test. For that student, taking the general assessment measures the effects of the blindness, not the student's skills and understanding. But with the accommodation of a Braille text, the blind student who uses Braille can respond to test items and be measured against the standards expected of all students. A student who has difficulty reading due to a processing disability may need the accommodation of having the instructions read or perhaps extended time to be able to show what he or she knows and is able to do. To measure how well *all* students are doing, states and districts must find a way for *all* students to fairly show what they know and are able to do.

By law (see Box 1.6), and in practice, states and districts have defined the following options as the ways students participate in the assessment system:

- Participation in the general assessment, typically a large-scale assessment of some type
- Participation in the general assessment with accommodations to allow students to show what they know
- Participation in alternate ways of assessing what students know and are able to do, commonly called *alternate assessment*

Alternate assessment is reserved for students who cannot, even with accommodations, participate in the general assessment. Very few students need alternate assessments—perhaps 1% to 2% of the total population of students, typically those with very significant disabilities.

The concept of accountability systems is similar. For *all* students to benefit from school reform efforts, we need to have multiple ways to determine *why* students are or are not being successful and multiple ways to determine *how* to improve results. For example, if we know from assessment results that a group of students is not doing well on mathematical problems at the Grade 8 level, we *may* have a curriculum problem to solve. On the other hand, if we find that many students in that group also have poor attendance rates, missing 9 or more days per semester, then the problem may require different or additional solutions. A school improvement team may do a school climate analysis or provide cultural training for staff; it may identify promising new instructional methods for engaging students in their own learning or perhaps begin new teacher-parent partnerships. IASA 1994 specifically requires that achievement results from assessments must be part of the accountability system, but it allows each state to determine other measures—such as attendance—to be included as well.

ALTERNATE ASSESSMENTS WITHIN ⊞ ASSESSMENT AND ACCOUNTABILITY SYSTEMS

As we said earlier, an alternate assessment is a way to measure the performance of students who are unable to participate in general large-scale assessments used by a district or state. Alternate assessments provide a mechanism for students with even the most significant disabilities to be included in the assessment system. Alternate assessments are designed to increase the capacity of large-scale assessment systems to show how a school, district, or state is doing in terms of student performance and to ensure that all students are included in the accountability system as we improve results.

In other words, although alternate assessments often give us good information about each individual student, that is not the primary purpose for using them. The primary purpose of alternate assessments in state or district assessment systems is accountability: to increase the capacity of the state to create information on how a school, district, or state is doing in terms of overall student performance. From that information, schools can make broad policy decisions that improve schooling practices so all students are successful.

Performance on alternate assessments must be reported with other scores in the assessment system. By including *all* scores in the assessment system, then *all* students can also benefit from the accountability system. But for the scores from the alternate assessments to be included in the assessment and accountability systems, it is important to remember that the assessments are measuring progress toward standards.

We believe it is essential to view alternate assessments as an alternate way of assessing progress toward the *same* standards as all other students are working toward. This is not an alternate-standards approach. Accountability systems are designed to improve results as measured against high standards—thus we believe alternate assessments must be linked to the high standards that are expected for *all* students. We discuss how this works in Chapter 2.

Among assumptions that might be considered the foundation of alternate assessments (Ysseldyke & Olsen, 1997) are that the alternate assessments focus on authentic skills and on assessing experiences in community and other real-life environments and that alternate assessments should measure integrated skills across settings. The actual administration of alternate assessments is addressed in Chapter 6.

ALL MEANS *ALL* ⊞

State and federal education laws clearly and consistently indicate that all students must be included in state and district assessment systems either through participation in general assessments, with or without accommodations, or through participation in alternate assessments. Reasons why this participation of all students with disabilities, including those with the most significant disabilities, is so important were discussed in our earlier book, *Testing Students with Disabilities* (Thurlow, Elliott, & Ysseldyke, 1998), and are worth summarizing here. All students need to be included in assessment systems

- *For an accurate picture of education:* It is not possible to get an accurate picture of a district's or state's educational system if some of the students are removed from the picture. Alternate assessments allow districts and states to include virtually 100% of students in the assessment picture.
- *To make accurate comparisons:* Once assessment results are reported, the reports are compared among schools, districts, and states. For accurate comparisons to be made, all students need to be included by all schools, districts, and states. If not, a district that tested less than 90% of its students would probably show scores that are not comparable to a district that tested nearly 100% of its students.
- *For students with disabilities to benefit from reforms:* Often, the results of statewide assessments are used to make district and state educational policy decisions about the curriculum or resource allocation. When students are not included in assessments, their performance does not influence policy decisions that may affect their education. Only by including all students can the educational system address the needs of all students.
- *To avoid unintended consequences of exclusion:* If there are significant consequences associated with assessments (e.g., school accreditation, student graduation), one of the unintended consequences might be increased referrals to special education. Another consequence has been an increase in the number of students retained in the grade preceding a test grade, presumably to keep them from being included in testing until they are more mature or ready for the test. For example, if a statewide test is given to 3rd graders, some students who are expected to perform poorly might be retained in 2nd grade.
- *To promote high expectations:* The most frequent reason students with disabilities are excluded from assessment is that they are not expected to do well. These low expectations can pervade a student's entire educational career, resulting in lowered standards for what a student is taught and expected to achieve. Low expectations are often related to low achievement. And for students who have significant disabilities, low expectations are often the norm.
- *To meet legal requirements:* There are now several federal mandates that require the participation of all students in statewide assessments. Primary among these are IDEA and IASA.

⊞ DOES *ALL* INCLUDE LARA?

In the past, Lara, the 8th grader introduced in the Preface, was completely excluded from the district and state accountability system and from any school improvement efforts. She was, in the terms of one of her teachers, a "set-aside kid." There was no standardized way of measuring what she could do that was aligned with what was expected of anyone else. As you will see throughout this book, Lara and everyone involved in her life benefited from her participation in the state assessment system. Lara became a real person to many who had viewed her simply as a case in the past. Her district benefited because it had a complete picture of the results of high expectations for every student. Now, the dis-

Figure 1.1. Steps to the Development and Administration of Alternate Assessments

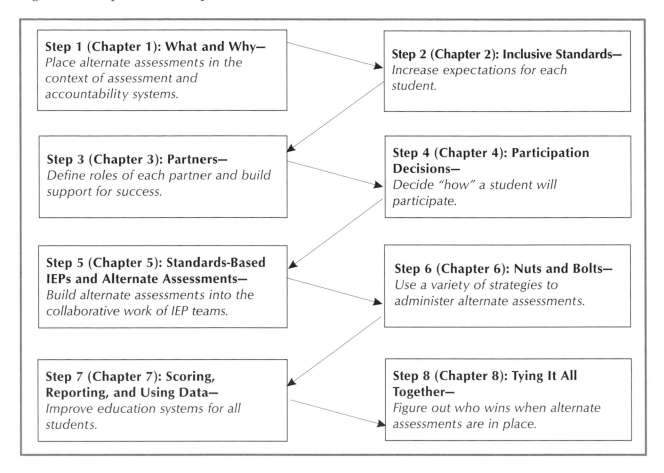

Step 1 (Chapter 1): What and Why—
Place alternate assessments in the context of assessment and accountability systems.

Step 2 (Chapter 2): Inclusive Standards—
Increase expectations for each student.

Step 3 (Chapter 3): Partners—
Define roles of each partner and build support for success.

Step 4 (Chapter 4): Participation Decisions—
Decide "how" a student will participate.

Step 5 (Chapter 5): Standards-Based IEPs and Alternate Assessments—
Build alternate assessments into the collaborative work of IEP teams.

Step 6 (Chapter 6): Nuts and Bolts—
Use a variety of strategies to administer alternate assessments.

Step 7 (Chapter 7): Scoring, Reporting, and Using Data—
Improve education systems for all students.

Step 8 (Chapter 8): Tying It All Together—
Figure out who wins when alternate assessments are in place.

trict could make decisions based on comprehensive information that included all students.

Lara's story provides clues to the best answers to the tough questions asked at the beginning of each chapter. Her team was able to use alternate assessments to increase expectations and dramatically improve her success. To help you comply with alternate assessment requirements and do what is best for *your* students, we have organized this book to provide what you need to know and what you need to do in each chapter. We use students' stories—students like Lara, Becca, Tony, and several others as well—to illustrate how what you know and can do with alternate assessments will help your students reach high expectations for learning.

OVERVIEW OF THE BOOK ✖

One of our goals in writing this book has been to provide a comprehensive guide to the development and administration of alternate assessments. We started with a list of steps and soon found that the steps became chapters. So, if you read this book from cover to cover, you will get a complete picture of the entire alternate assessment process. Figure 1.1 shows a graphic summary of each step. We also give you a summary of how the steps are addressed in each chapter.

Step 1: What and Why

Make sure everyone involved with the administration of alternate assessments has some understanding of standards and accountability systems before they are introduced to the nuts and bolts of alternate assessments. Without this context, alternate assessments are just "one more thing the state is making us do." Chapter 1 provides this context of laws, beliefs, and practices.

Step 2: Inclusive Standards

Consider how *all* of the students in your school can work toward the same standards and how their progress can be measured. Then, consider how students with significant disabilities are working toward broad standards and how alternate assessments can measure their progress. You may find that your students are not getting as many opportunities to learn to the standards as they should. Can your students learn at higher levels? Can you expect more of them? How can you help them stretch to higher levels against the state or district standards? This step is a good place to examine your current expectations very carefully. Chapter 2 guides you through the process of thinking about how high standards apply to *all* students and how alternate assessments measure progress toward those standards.

Step 3: Partners

Identify who can best support the students you serve as they work toward standards. Most students with significant disabilities have many resources and people who help them during each day—from related services, to community supports at job sites or living skills sites, to general education classrooms and the home. Identifying who can support each student in instruction and in assessment is a very important step. Chapter 3, "Alternate Assessment Partners," helps you think about who can support students as they work toward standards and participate in alternate assessments.

Step 4: Participation Decisions

Work with each student's IEP team to make annual decisions about how a student will participate in assessment and accountability systems—in general assessments with no accommodations, in general assessments with accommodations, or in alternate assessments. Chapter 4, "Assessment Participation Decisions," guides IEP teams through this important decision-making process.

Step 5: Standards-Based IEPs and Alternate Assessments

IEP teams have an opportunity to integrate standards and assessments into IEPs. Students can also use standards to work toward transition plans. Use the IEP form to document standards-based instruction and assessment decisions. With the team, design a plan to allow every partner to share in the instruction and the assessment of standards and work together as the plan is carried out. Chapter 5 shows how the IEP process and inclusive standards fit together. This chapter also identifies ways standards-based reform enriches transition services for students who are moving from school to adult life.

Step 6: Nuts and Bolts

The nuts and bolts of gathering high-quality assessment data and assembling them in appropriate ways is the core of the process of alternate assessment, but gathering high-quality data depends on the thoughtful preparatory work in the preceding steps. States and districts vary on how data will be assembled and handled, so what you do specifically to gather and prepare the data will vary as well. Chapter 6, "The Nuts and Bolts of Alternate Assessment Administration," looks at a variety of assessment strategies and ways to compile assessment data.

Step 7: Scoring, Reporting, and Using Data

Once alternate assessment data are gathered, state, district, and school administrators must have all assessments scored and then report to the public and to the parents how their school is doing. How your school and district use the data is very important. All states are working with districts to identify school improvement planning processes that help schools take the information from student assessments and improve curriculum and instruction so that more students can be successful. In Chapter 7, "Scoring, Reporting, and Using Alternate Assessment Data," we think through how to ensure that data from alternate assessments are used to improve schools as well as to improve instruction for individual students.

Step 8: Tying It All Together

After completing an assessment year and before moving into the next year, take time to check out the benefits and challenges, not only of the standards and assessment systems but also the benefits of the reform effort for students and everyone who serves them. In Chapter 8, we return to the big-picture view of how to ensure that inclusive assessment and accountability systems are good for all students.

Each of these chapters relates to what we believe is possible for students with the most significant disabilities. Although we have shown how standards-based reform has the potential to improve outcomes for all students, we can't really convince anyone who truly believes these students can't learn or can't learn in measurable ways. As the story of Lara suggests, sometimes it takes success with a real student to be convinced that standards-based instruction and alternate assessments can be good for students, and in the process, many teachers have found that it is good for their professional growth as well.

We relate stories about students like Lara, Becca, and Tony in the chapters ahead and see how they each may benefit from standards-based reform. It is also important to apply the information in the rest of the book to students *you* know and work with in order for *you* to get answers for students you care about. At the end of the book, we pose the tough questions asked at the beginning of each chapter again, and again ask *you* to answer them for yourself.

All students means *all* students. That is a requirement. *What* standards each state and district sets for all students is a state and district decision, although for federally funded programs, the requirement is that those standards are higher than in the past. *How* schools help all children reach high standards is flexible; *how* schools measure progress is a state and district decision. Remember to gather the information you need to tailor our suggestions to your own school, district, state, and most important, your students.

2

Inclusive Standards

High Expectations for All Students

TOUGH QUESTIONS

What are the state standards? I've never been expected to use them with my students.

How does the alternate assessment fit into district and state standards? Most of the students I serve will never be able to read or do math!

My students are learning functional skills. How does that relate to standards-based learning and subject area knowledge and skills?

I f all children can learn, if all children can thrive in an atmosphere of high expectations, and if all children can be successful, what is it we "expect" of them? And can we truly expect the same of all children? What does being successful mean for students like Lara, Becca, and Tony?

Content and performance standards give us commonly defined goals, commonly accepted targets of what children should know and be able to do. It is clear in federal law that all students receiving federally funded educational services must be held to challenging standards. It is also clear that students vary in their performance levels—some students learn to higher levels than others, even when all students have an opportunity to learn to high levels. So how do we sort that out to be sure we have high expectations for every child? And how can state- and district-defined content and performance standards help us build those high expectations into a student's IEP? These are the questions we hope to answer in this chapter.

Same Standards for Lara?

Before Lara was included in standards and alternate assessments, her IEP goals consisted mostly of physical maintenance—things that were done *to* her, rather than things she was learning. When a decision was made to include Lara in the alternate assessment, the first step was to figure out how she could learn toward standards. Members of her team took a hard look at her instructional day and had to ask themselves some difficult questions about her isolated placement and lack of instruction.

For Lara to learn toward standards, her team knew that they needed to collaborate with the general education staff. The special education coordinator met with a few interested general education staff and explained that Lara was going to begin working toward standards. Together, they discussed where in general education classrooms, at home, and in the community Lara could work toward the same standards as the other students, in ways that she learned best.

The special education staff at Lara's school was fortunate in that standards have been implemented in their district for about 7 years, and all staff had become familiar with them—including special educators—and understood how standards could be met across disciplines. Standards were "old language" for some members of Lara's team. So training for special educators did not have to start with "what are standards?" They could begin with the standards currently in place and expand the performance indicators to include Lara.

Lara's team decided to have her work on responding to the directive, "look at me," by making eye contact with the speaker. They also decided to work on having her touch a switch. By looking at some of the performance indicators in the reading standard, her team got the idea that by combining Lara's ability to look at something with her ability to hit a button, they could actually teach her some reading skills. They took a book and put icons with an embedded switch in the text electronically connected to an audiotape. When they were reading with Lara, they hoped to teach her to hit the icon whenever it appeared, thus activating the audiotape that would then "read" the text for that page.

At the time they developed the plan, they weren't sure Lara could control her movements or even visually track well enough to recognize the icon. At first, Lara cried—she hated the prompting and she hated the demands placed on her, where none had ever been before. But over the course of the year, Lara was able to "read" several books with no physical or verbal prompting. It took persistence, but the team now expects Lara to learn, and it is able to account for her progress, both on her IEP and on the alternate assessment.

CONTENT STANDARDS DEFINED ▓

Content standards are educational targets for students to learn toward. They are not instructional curricula or technical documents used by teachers to guide day-to-day instruction. Teachers ensure that students work toward content standards by using a range of instructional strategies that they select based on their students' varied needs and goals. In most states, the content standards represent extensive planning, discussion, and interaction with administrators, teachers, and school partners, as well as state and local policymakers, business partners, and community members. In addition, several national and state documents on standards setting have been produced, and most states continue to refine their standards approaches as more is learned from research and practice.

The discussions these groups have had about standards tend to focus on these topics:

- What do we believe all children should know and be able to do?
- What are essential skills for success in today's world?

Although the answers vary somewhat across the states, there is some general agreement.

First, all states that have standards address the need for basic skills in literacy and numeracy. Literacy typically means skills and understanding in communication areas, including reading, writing, listening, and speaking. Numeracy typically addresses the ability to make sense of money, numbers, and spatial and linear relationships, for example. In many states, other traditional content areas, such as social studies, science, and the arts, have been addressed by content standards as well. In some states, these content standards are general statements of what every student should know and be able to do to function well in the 21st century. In other states, specific knowledge and skills within a field are defined—more a curricular definition than general content. These distinctions are important in how students with significant disabilities are included in standards.

Second, in our rapidly changing world, many groups that identified standards for all children to know and be able to do have emphasized the ability to apply knowledge and skills in new settings and the ability to seek out new knowledge and skills. In many states, these skills and understanding focus on methods of inquiry or the concepts and processes across traditional academic disciplines.

Last, some states have added standards that help students link across their traditional academic disciplines with skills to seek out and apply knowledge in a third area, such as career-vocational linkages, citizenship, resource management, or use of technology. Table 2.1 shows one state's comprehensive set of learning areas, each of which contains several standards.

As you work on alternate assessments with your students, you need to become very familiar with the standards in your own state. Most state education agency Web sites contain basic information about the state standards, and most states and districts are providing continuing training on the standards. Be sure that you become involved with

TABLE 2.1	Example of One State's Learning Areas
Read, Listen, and View	Write and Speak
Arts and Literature	Mathematical Applications
Inquiry (research skills)	Scientific Applications
People and Cultures (social studies)	Decision Making
Resource Management	World Languages

the training. You need to understand your state's approach thoroughly to be able to effectively involve the students you serve in this reform. Remember that the CCSSO maintains a Web page that links to every state education agency (*http://www.ccsso.org/seamenu.html*). A comprehensive online resource on state standards is the Mid-Continent Regional Education Laboratory. Their standards Web pages begin at *http://www.mcrel.org/products/standards/index.asp*

⠶ HOW CONTENT STANDARDS APPLY TO ALL STUDENTS

Does the need to have basic communication skills and understanding of numbers, the ability to apply knowledge in multiple settings, or the need to find ways to contribute to society through career or vocation, citizenship, or technology apply to all students? By thinking about these questions, we can better understand how content standards apply to all students. These three kinds of skills and abilities are typically included in state content standards:

- Basic content area knowledge, skills, and understanding, particularly in the areas of literacy and numeracy
- The ability to transfer knowledge to new settings and seek out new learning
- The ability to apply what is learned to career or vocational paths, citizenship, resource management, or technology

Aren't these appropriate outcomes for all students? These skills and abilities are skills and abilities needed by academically gifted students, by typical students, by students with mild disabilities, and by students with the most significant disabilities.

Will the way we teach all these students vary? Yes! And do some students need alternate ways of showing us what they know and how they are able to do these things? Yes! And do students vary on the level to which they perform along the path to the highest standards? Yes! But all students can work toward these same high standards (see Box 2.1). If students are not learning along the path to the standards, it is the learning plan that needs changing, *not* the standards.

Although all students will work toward the same high standards, there are multiple ways of observing and measuring their progress. That brings us to the discussion of performance standards.

Box 2.1

— *Guidance on Standards, Assessments, and Accountability That Supplements the Elementary & Secondary Education Act as Amended by the Improving America's Schools Act of 1994, P.L. 103-382 (1997)*

"What if assessments being used to measure the performance of all students do not measure what students with disabilities are currently learning in their programs? While some students with disabilities may need modified instructional approaches, generally all students need to be working toward the same challenging standards." (II. Assessments, Questions #43, p. 10 of 16)

PERFORMANCE STANDARDS DEFINED ✖

Performance standards are the expected achievement level for state- and district-defined content standards. In a nutshell,

- Content standards define what students are expected to know and be able to do.
- Performance standards describe the quality of performance expected for proficiency on the content standards.
- Benchmarks are specific examples of the academic standards at each grade level or in each academic course.
- Performance indicators are measurable, observable skills expected at each grade level or in each academic course.

If a state or district has defined a content standard as "the student can jump," then the performance standard would define "how high or how far the student can jump" when the student has mastered the task. The benchmark would tell us what we should expect at checkpoints along the learning path to achieving the standards, and performance indicators help us measure the student's progress.

Title I legislation is very clear that all students are expected to learn the same content. It is also clear that all students will be held to the same high standards of performance. And it is also clear that all students "can and will vary in their performance levels" (see Box 2.2).

HOW PERFORMANCE STANDARDS ✖
APPLY TO ALL STUDENTS

How can a state's or district's performance standards apply to students with the most significant disabilities? Each student is expected to reach performance levels that are higher than they have been before, even though, as stated in Box 2.2, "students can and will vary in their performance levels." Performance levels can be raised using "a wide range of instructional methods and strategies." Many states have chosen to "expand" their content standards to include very fundamental skills, which have several names across states and districts, such as *basic, access, essential, foundational,* or *functional*

Box 2.2

— *Guidance on Standards, Assessments, and Accountability That Supplements the Elementary & Sec-ondary Education Act as Amended by the Improving America's Schools Act of 1994, P.L. 103-382 (1997)*

"What does it mean to say that standards apply to all children? Whether standards apply statewide or districtwide, all students within that State or district must be held to the same challenging standards. In other words, All students including . . . students with diverse learning needs, are expected to learn the same general high-quality content, rather than a separate curriculum for certain students, although a wide range of instructional methods and strategies could be used. All students are held to the same high standards of performance, regardless of the assessment instrument used. Students can and will vary in their performance levels—some students will learn more than others. However, the perfor-mance levels all students need to reach in order to 'meet the standard' will be set much higher than at present." (I. Content and Performance Standards, Questions #12, p. 7 of 8)

---

skills. These skills are aligned with standards; that is, mastery of these skills leads students toward the achievement of high standards. Some states require students to learn particular skills as indicators of progress toward standards. Other states offer examples of skills or performance indicators and then invite IEP teams to select a student's performance indicators from the examples or develop their own. *Selecting performance indicators that effectively demonstrate a student's progress toward standards is critical to the participation of each student with significant disabilities in standards-based reform.*

We have used several terms in the preceding paragraphs, terms that vary considerably across states. Our definitions of these terms are summarized in Table 2.2. Remember that it is very important for you to become familiar with the terms used in your district or state.

How do expanded standards or performance indicators help include all students, and how do they relate to alternate assessment? The purpose of alternate assessments is to assess the progress of students with significant disabilities toward standards. Nearly all states have developed educational standards for students to meet. Most of these standards have been designed with grade-level benchmarks. Many states have expanded their standards to include functional skills as performance indicators, thus including all students within the same set of standards. What we suggest here is that by keeping students in the same set of standards and adjusting performance indicators to appropriate levels, the highest possible expectations are encouraged, challenging the students to the highest possible outcomes (see Box 2.3).

⊞ CONTENT AND PERFORMANCE STANDARDS IN PRACTICE

Students with significant disabilities can reach higher levels of achievement by linking their learning, which is documented in their IEP goals, to the standards our society expects of all students. With partners in teaching and learning on the IEP team and beyond into the school, community, and home, we can work together to discover new ways for each student to be more successful. For example, IEP teams work to blend the unique

TABLE 2.2   **Important Terms**

Content standards define what students are expected to know and be able to do.

Performance standards describe what students must do to demonstrate proficiency at a specific level on the content standards.

Benchmarks are specific examples of the academic standards at each grade level or in each academic course.

Performance indicators are examples or an assigned set of measurable or observable skills that show progress toward standards.

Expanded standards or performance indicators are standards or performance indicators that are expanded beyond grade-level benchmarks to show every student's progress toward content standards, no matter how significant the student's disabilities. This expansion includes age-appropriate functional skills that become the "high expectation" bridge between the state content and performance standards and the needs and abilities of students with the most significant disabilities. The term *extended* is used instead of *expanded* in some states.

Age-appropriate functional skills is a phrase familiar to special educators. These are skills students need for meaningful participation within their communities. These skills, called *access* or *basic* or *essential* or *foundational* skills in different places across the country, become the performance indicators that show progress toward standards. Some states have categorized these skills into learning areas, such as vocational, independent living, recreation, and community participation.

Box 2.3

▬ *A Caveat on Separate Standards*

Some states have completely separate standards or no common standards for students with significant disabilities. This builds an assumption that these students do not profit from access to the general education curriculum. It also makes it very difficult to include these students in an accountability system that holds schools responsible for student progress toward standards. How do you then improve schooling for this group? And how do you ensure that every student is benefiting from high expectations? Here is what Title I Guidance tells us about separate standards:

▬ *Guidance on Standards, Assessments, and Accountability That Supplements the Elementary & Secondary Education Act as Amended by the Improving America's Schools Act of 1994, P.L. 103-382 (1997)*

"Assessments for Title I purposes focus on whether the yearly performance of each Local Education Agency (LEA) and school served under Title I is enabling all children served to meet the State's student performance standards. It is important that students with disabilities be included in these assessments because they are expected to meet the same standards as other students." (II. Assessments, Questions #42, p. 10 of 16)

Figure 2.1. Bridge Between IEP Goals and Standards

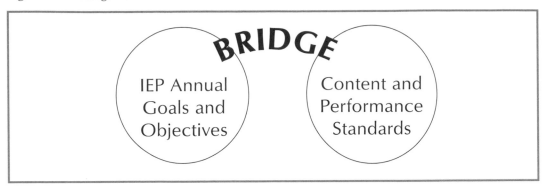

needs and strengths of the student into a year-by-year plan for progress. What we are adding now is a bridge from those IEP goals to the general education standards, as shown in Figure 2.1.

The decision about how alternate assessment participants can work toward standards varies as a result of the type of standards required by a state or district. Some states and districts focus very narrowly on specific academic standards, whereas others take a broader approach and include many functional or life skills within their standards for all students. For some states, even though the content standards assessed by an alternate assessment are the same as those assessed by the general large-scale assessment, the indicators of progress are different, often focusing on functional life skills rather than on specific academic skills. Performance standards may also be defined differently, to differentiate between the types of benchmarks and indicators expected at specific grade levels and the indicators measured by the alternate assessment. See Box 2.4.

Remember that highly committed stakeholder groups in most states have developed the state standards through a long and carefully planned sequence of activities. Even though many states will continue to review and refine their standards long into the future, these standards represent what it means to "be successful" in your state. Students with disabilities ultimately will be measured by the same criteria, whether in the classroom or in real life. *The indicators of performance used to measure success may vary for individual students, but the ability to communicate well; to understand numbers, shapes, and patterns; and to apply that knowledge to life roles is as much a measure of success for the person with significant disabilities as it is for anyone else.*

Here are six principles to consider in working toward standards-based instruction and assessment for all students:

1. Bottom line—the purpose of special education services is to give students the support they need to work toward high standards. IEP team members need to think about and discuss the importance of achieving high standards—the "bottom line" in planning with a student. If the team agrees that the purpose of all efforts is to help students advance as far as possible toward achieving personal goals and high standards, then the lines between general and special education blur, and goals naturally address standards.

2. Standards-based instruction helps focus and give direction to a student's special education services and supports. It reflects student learning—and ensures that educational goals cover areas that have been determined to be beneficial to the lives of students both in and out of school.

Box 2.4

▬ *Peer Reviewer Guidance for Evaluating Evidence of Final Assessments Under Title I of the Elementary & Secondary Education Act, P.L. 103-382 (1999)*

"Typically, alternate assessments incorporate more fundamental changes to testing conditions, such as using an entirely different format for the assessment (e.g., a portfolio system instead of on-demand tests) or assessing content standards that are changed in some way (e.g., expanded standards with different performance descriptors)." (Part IB. Inclusion, p. 14)

3. Standards-based curriculum in general education gives students with disabilities opportunities to work toward standards in many ways. As educational reform moves us from teacher-centered and curriculum-based systems to student-centered and standards-based systems, flexibility in strategies for achieving standards for all students is necessary. This gives students with disabilities many more opportunities to achieve standards at their highest individual level.

4. Students who are working toward the same standards as other students are more likely to be included in activities with general education students. For example, a high school student with disabilities who is learning to throw garbage away and re-cycle cans (working toward standards in math and science through resource management and problem solving) could participate in a recycling service project in a general education environmental science class. A 6-year-old student with disabilities learning to listen quietly (working toward an English Language Arts standard) could participate in story time in the library with the rest of her 1st-grade class.

5. Basing IEP goals on standards increases the opportunities that students with disabilities have to leave their special education classrooms and learn across multiple settings. For each goal, it is important to bridge across learning opportunities available in school, home, and community settings. The student learning to engage in listening quietly to a story could also work on the skill during story time at the public library and at home with a sibling, parent, relative, or babysitter. The student working on recycling could practice as a member of a scout troop, a church youth group, and at home.

6. Assessing the progress of all students toward standards makes us all accountable for the progress students with disabilities make toward their IEP goals—if those goals are standards-based. Consider Lara, for example. Her previous IEP goals fo-cused mainly on maintenance, on what adults would do to keep her healthy and comfortable. There was no focus at all on what she could learn, because no one really thought she could learn. Then, standards came into play, with the requirement that Lara participate in an alternate assessment. Well, you can't participate in an assessment if you haven't learned anything that can be assessed. Thus began the search for something Lara could learn that would show progress toward standards and could be assessed. Unfortunately, Lara was already 14 years old. This process could have started when Lara was very young so that by the time this first state or district assessment rolled around, she would have already been well prepared to participate in an assessment of her progress toward standards.

✖ HOW TO GET STUDENTS WITH DISABILITIES INVOLVED IN STANDARDS-BASED INSTRUCTION

Often, special educators have been excluded from discussions about standards and have not become familiar with them, thinking standards had nothing to do with them. We talked to a district person who set up a task force to work on getting students with disabilities involved in standards-based instruction who said, "At the first meeting of about 15 task force members, we realized that only three of the special educators had any familiarity with the standards, so we had to start at the very beginning." That may need to be done in your district.

The first step in getting students with disabilities involved in standards-based instruction is to become familiar with your district and state standards. This is a big step for many special educators and related-services staff who may have been excluded from training and development on standards in the past. When assumptions are made that a group of students will be excluded from a district's standards, assessments, and accountability system, assumptions are also made that the people who work with those students have no need to know about this system. These assumptions can further separate the education of these students and reduce even more the perceived value of their education.

So how can special educators and related-services providers learn about standards? There are several things that can be done. First, read about the standards. Find out what written information was distributed to general educators, and get a copy. Districts usually have some type of standards coordinator. This would be the person to ask. Asking the standards coordinator for information about the district's standards would be a first step in the door to being included.

States generally have their information about standards posted on their Web sites. This is another good place to get a broad view of the standards required by your state. Talk to general educators to get their understanding of the district's standards, and find out what types of training they have had and what's coming up in the future. Get on the general education mailing list for information about standards, assessment, and training.

The goal of this information-gathering process is to find out what the standards are and what types of benchmarks, learning expectations, or performance indicators (different places call these different things) students need to accomplish to show that they are making progress toward those standards.

The next step is to find out what has been done in your district and state to help alternate assessment participants progress toward standards. For example, some states have expanded their standards to include indicators of progress that are functional or life skills oriented. Some states have a list of "essential" skills that students need to meet before working toward grade-level benchmarks. Some districts and states base their performance indicators on an established functional curriculum or adaptive behavior scale. Every state and district has something that shows what alternate assessment participants are assessed on. This information should be available in written form and may also be posted on a state's or district's Web site. Because alternate assessments are now required, nearly every state is in the process of statewide training that includes information about indicators of progress toward standards as described in this chapter. Get this information. It is critical for building standards-based instruction for alternate assessment participants.

SELECTING STANDARDS TO WORK TOWARD ❈

Selecting what standards a student should work toward depends somewhat on a state's or district's requirements. For example, in some states, there are several standards in the area of Mathematics with various requirements about how many are required and how many are elective. Also, with each standard comes a list of skills, performance indicators, or learning expectations (they are called different things in different places). Looking through these may also help an IEP team's selection of standards to work toward. The selection of goals, skills, or performance indicators that show progress toward standards may take place in a variety of ways. These are described in Chapter 5.

Remember that bridge illustrated back in Figure 2.1? Here is an example of how a connection can be made between a functional skill that is documented as an IEP goal for Tony (the 6th grader introduced in Chapter 1) and his state's standards:

Tony's IEP goal: *Tony will turn on his boom box by touching a switch on the lapboard on his wheelchair.*

Tony's state assesses standards in these areas:

English Language Arts	Mathematics
Reading	Number operations and concepts
Writing	Geometry
Speaking	Measurement
Listening	Algebraic concepts and relationships
	Tools and technology
	Problem solving and mathematical reasoning

At first, Tony's IEP team could not see a connection between his goal and the standards. But, as they thought more about it, they realized that Tony was communicating a desire—which indicated progress toward a "speaking" standard. They also realized that Tony was using assistive technology—an indicator of progress toward a "tools and technology" standard.

Let's take this exercise a step further. Using your district or state information about standards, inclusive standards if they exist, make a chart like the one in Table 2.3, with your student's IEP goals listed on the left side and the standards, or at least the categories or areas in which the standards fit, on the right side.

With a student's current IEP goals listed on the left and an understanding of the standards listed on the right, try to match them by letters and numbers (see Table 2.4 for an example). Here, it is very important to know what standards are in each category. For example, without knowing what an actual geometry standard looks like, it would be very difficult (without any experience teaching mathematics) to figure out how any of these goals could fit that area. So let's use a more specific example of a geometry standard. One state has a geometry standard that states, "The student will demonstrate, construct, communicate, and apply the properties of geometric shapes and spatial sense to connect geometry with problem-solving situations."

Well, that still doesn't get me very far if I don't know much about the properties of geometric shapes. I get additional clues from a general education math teacher who de-

TABLE 2.3   Matching IEP Goals to Standards

IEP Goals	*Categories of Standards*
1. Touch a switch to turn on a stereo.	a. Reading
2. Pass out milk to classmates at morning break.	b. Writing
3. Touch a computer screen to create and send E-mail messages.	c. Listening
	d. Speaking
4. Open a can using an electric can opener.	e. Number Operations and Concepts
5. Follow a picture recipe to make a sandwich.	f. Geometry
6. Stock shelves (e.g., groceries, auto parts) with items by shape or symbol.	g. Measurement
7. Indicate when a cup is full or empty.	h. Algebraic Concepts and Relationships
8. Copy personal information (i.e., name, phone number).	i. Tools and Technology
9. Use an eye blink signal to communicate "yes" or "no."	j. Problem Solving and Mathematical Reasoning
10. Determine whether a personal wheelchair will fit through a space.	
11. Recognize or identify safety symbols.	
12. Use an alarm clock to get up at a designated time.	
13. Use cash to purchase an item.	
14. Listen attentively to a concert, play, or speaker.	

scribes the student learning expectations or indicators of progress toward that standard in general education. For example,

- Sort, classify, and construct geometric shapes or figures and objects using a variety of manipulatives.
- Demonstrate spatial awareness (positional relationship, size, direction, area, volume, etc.).

You will quickly find that more than one match can be found for most goals. Are there any goals with no matches? If there are, are these really goals a student is working toward, or are they health-maintenance activities done by someone else?

Notice in Table 2.4 that every goal fits at least one standard area, and most connect to more than one. After becoming familiar with the standards in the geometry area, we found that at least eight of the goals listed could help a student make progress toward a standard in geometry. These included opening a can, stocking shelves, indicating when a cup is full or empty, and determining whether a wheelchair will fit through a space. But it also included items such as touching a switch to turn on a stereo, following a picture recipe, recognizing safety symbols, or using a computer touch screen, because geometric shapes are so prevalent in each of these activities. Any time a student uses

TABLE 2.4   Examples of Matches Between IEP Goals and Standards

IEP Goals	Categories of Standards
1. Touch a switch to turn on a stereo. a, c, f, g, i, j	a. Reading
2. Pass out milk to classmates at morning break. c, d, e, g, h, j	b. Writing
3. Touch a computer screen to create and send E-mail messages. a, b, c, f, i	c. Listening d. Speaking
4. Open a can using an electric can opener. f, g, i, j	e. Number Operations and Concepts
5. Follow a picture recipe to make a sandwich. a, e, f, j	f. Geometry
6. Stock shelves (e.g., groceries, auto parts) with items by shape or symbol. f, g, h, j	g. Measurement
7. Indicate when a cup is full or empty. c, d, f, g, j	h. Algebraic Concepts and Relationships i. Tools and Technology
8. Copy personal information (i.e., name, phone number). a, b, e	j. Problem Solving and Mathematical Reasoning
9. Use an eye blink signal to communicate "yes" or "no." c, d, i	
10. Determine if personal wheelchair will fit through a space. f, g, i	
11. Recognize/identify safety symbols. a, c, f	
12. Use an alarm clock to get up at a designated time. c, e, g, i, j	
13. Use cash to purchase an item. a, c, d, e, h, j	

assistive technology, that student is working toward standards in tools and technology, and every skill that requires a student to make a decision helps him or her work toward standards in problem solving and mathematical reasoning.

Every state's standards are different, and districts often have standards in addition to those required by a state. At this time, however, most states are only assessing progress toward standards in the areas of English Language Arts (generally including reading and writing) and Mathematics. Alternate assessments are just that—alternates to the assessments, so they only require assessment in the areas currently required by a state or district. However, IEPs should reflect progress toward the same standards as those expected of all other students. This means a student's goals may reflect progress toward standards in several areas. Developing and documenting standards-based IEP goals is addressed in detail in Chapter 6.

3

Alternate Assessment Partners

TOUGH QUESTIONS

Are special education teachers responsible for the whole process of administering alternate assessments?

What happens if parents refuse to have their children participate in state assessments, including alternate assessments?

School psychologists administer most of our placement assessments. Do alternate assessments need to be administered by them, too?

Paraprofessionals are unable to attend IEP meetings in our district. Because they are heavily involved in the education of students with disabilities, can they still be involved in alternate assessments?

One of the issues that has arisen in the initial implementation of alternate assessment systems is the fear of special educators that they will get "stuck holding the bag" for a comprehensive and time-consuming new assessment system. The implementation of alternate assessments needs to be carried out through a partnership among many people, just as the education of children with disabilities needs a variety of partners to be successful. Several of these partners are members of a student's IEP team, whereas others may assist in the assessment process in other ways. Paraprofessionals, for example, who are rarely included in the development of IEPs (often because of scheduling issues), may be responsible for teaching and assessing skills that help students work toward standards and may also be involved in the alternate-assessment process. School district assessment coordinators may be responsible for gathering completed alternate assessments for scoring, just as they are responsible for gathering the general tests that are included in state and district assessment systems. And who could be more important in this process than the parents of the students? Yet they may receive little useful information to help them to understand the different ways students can participate in assessments and why this participation is so important. In this chapter, we discuss the roles of these and other partners through each stage of the assessment process, from instructing students within a standards-based system, to participation decision making, to the administration, compilation, scoring, and use of alternate assessment data.

Who Are the Partners for Lara's Alternate Assessment?

The concept of alternate assessment was first presented to Lara's parents at an IEP meeting. Their initial response was, "No. We don't want her stressed. We don't want her out of the special education room. We don't want her part of this. Where do we sign?" Lara's dad said, "Lara is not comfortable in general education rooms. Her peers aren't welcoming her." It didn't take the special education staff long to realize that they had probably taken too big of a leap too soon. The staff decided to meet with Lara's parents more informally to give them more information before another team meeting was held. Later, over lunch, the staff and parents talked about educational standards and how Lara could participate in them, something that was completely new to Lara's parents. The special education teacher drew a picture of what the accountability system looked like in the past—with most kids in the middle of the system and Lara outside of the system.

Accountability system for student learning (education of most students)

Lara's education

Lara had never been counted and the school was never held accountable for what she learned. She never really had an opportunity to realize her potential. Lara's parents believed that Lara was so severely brain damaged that any voluntary response or control was not possible. They had never really seen their daughter as having a place in the system, either, because they had been told by medical doctors not to hope for any progress, ever. Lara's parents had resigned themselves to that prognosis over the years.

Other partners had limited expectations as well. Lara was in the unique position of having a full-time educational assistant at school. The assistant loved her dearly and enjoyed being with and caring for Lara. The downside was that she did not believe that Lara could learn anything and did all she could to protect Lara from experiencing any stress or difficulty. She talked baby talk to Lara and did everything for her. The assistant's favorite pastime during the school day was holding Lara in a rocking chair and reading romance novels out loud. Sometimes, they would both fall asleep in the chair.

When the IEP team started planning Lara's participation in the alternate assessment, they selected general education teachers, based on a willingness to welcome her. This was difficult because Lara made a lot of noise, and some teachers worried about the disruption. At first, general educators resisted participation on Lara's IEP team, because, for them, what was the point? She was not theirs; they didn't know her, and no one thought she could learn anything anyway.

To help general educators get more involved in Lara's instruction, the special education staff developed checklists to record observations. It was very simple—a recording sheet was attached to a clipboard on Lara's wheelchair, and the aide gave it to the teacher to check off at the end of the class. (There is an example of one of these checklists in Chapter 6). This showed the general education teacher what to look for very specifically and helped her to begin to "own" Lara as a member of her class. It may have been easier for the special education staff to do all of the record keeping, but they found it was a good way to get the general educators involved in educating Lara without overwhelming them. Once a couple of general education teachers got used to having Lara around, others became less reluctant to invite her to be part of their classes. For example, one day in the teachers' lounge, the photography teacher was heard talking about her positive experiences with Lara. A few days later, a social studies teacher was overheard saying that he heard that having Lara in class wasn't bad at all, and he was thinking about trying it.

Lara's special education staff used the law to pull in the school principal as a partner. They told the principal, "The state says we have to do this." The school counselor had no intention of including her in state assessments in "any way, shape, or form." The special education staff met with him and told him that Lara's name was included on the school enrollment list and that no student enrolled in the school was to be omitted from assessment participation—the lists were one and the same.

The school psychologist did not see a connection between her work, standards, and state assessments. The special education staff needed to work with her to help her figure out where Lara could begin her work toward standards and then assist in the development and implementation of reliable and valid assessment strategies for the alternate assessment.

In the past, the speech clinician would stop by Lara's classroom and say, "Oh, she's not talking yet? Well, I'll stop back next week." The clinician was from the "old school" where students were pulled from class and taken to a tiny room to work on articulation. He was not familiar with assistive technology or with alternate forms of communication. Once he became more involved on Lara's IEP team, he began to understand what Lara needed and advocate for the resources needed to get it for her.

Lara received both physical and occupational therapy, but it was only for physical maintenance, with everything being done to her and no opportunity to learn to do

Box 3.1

— *Amendments to the Individuals with Disabilities Education Act, P.L. 105-17 (1997)*

"(a) General. The public agency shall ensure that the IEP team for each child with a disability includes—

(1) The parents of the child;

(2) At least one regular education teacher of the child (if the child is, or may be, participating in the regular education environment);

(3) At least one special education teacher of the child, or if appropriate, at least one special education provider of the child;

(4) A representative of the public agency who—

   (i) Is qualified to provide, or supervise the provision of, specially designed instruction to meet the unique needs of children with disabilities;

   (ii) Is knowledgeable about the general curriculum; and

   (iii) Is knowledgeable about the availability of resources of the public agency;

(5) An individual who can interpret the instructional implications of evaluation results, who may be a member of the team described in paragraphs (a)(2) through (6) of this section;

(6) At the discretion of the parent or the agency, other individuals who have knowledge or special expertise regarding the child, including related services personnel as appropriate; and

(7) If appropriate, the child." (Sec. 300.344)

anything herself. Her goals in these areas were all for physical maintenance. It soon became clear that even though the therapy was needed, these therapists could also become part of Lara's instructional team and help figure out how she could work toward standards.

You can see from Lara's team that there is much more involved in preparing a student's partners for meaningful roles in the implementation of alternate assessments than just giving a 2-hour test on Tuesday. For the most part, students who need the alternate assessment are ones who most people believe not only can't be tested but also can't learn. It takes a lot of work to convince people that a student can learn. So for the rest of this chapter, we want to show you how to move partners all the way from "why bother, she can't learn anything anyway" to being excited about assessing a student's progress to see how far she has come and excited about coming up with more and more ways to improve her quality of life through education toward high standards.

There are several questions that come to bear in determining the roles and responsibilities of each partner, those required by law as shown in Box 3.1 and others, as students with disabilities receive instruction toward standards and then are assessed on their skills and progress through state and district assessments. These questions are addressed in the next section.

WHO BRINGS INFORMATION ABOUT ✖ STANDARDS AND ASSESSMENTS TO IEP TEAMS?

Often, in the past, standards and state assessments were not even mentioned at IEP team meetings for two primary reasons: (a) It was not believed that standards applied to most students with disabilities, and (b) there was no one on the team who knew anything about standards-based instruction. Now that a decision has been made that *all* students can and will work toward standards, it should be a given that standards are addressed with every student at every IEP meeting. As mentioned earlier in this book, however, special educators may not have been involved in the development or implementation of a district's standards and may not even have had ready access to information or participated in any training about standards. This is where the expertise of general educators is so important to an IEP team. General educators should have the background and content knowledge about standards to play an important role on an IEP team. They can help place a student's IEP goals within standards, and they can see where gaps exist—places where there are important standards that have not been addressed within a student's instructional program. They can also help special educators and other team members get up to speed in their own information base about standards. In addition, they can inform special educators and other team members about training on standards that they could participate in together in the future.

School administrators, counselors, and curriculum and assessment personnel may also bring important information about standards to IEP teams and set the expectation that each student will work toward standards. This does not mean that all of these people would need to attend every student's IEP meetings! It does mean that as members of a school community, everyone should be seen as a resource to everyone else and their expertise tapped freely as needed.

WHO BRINGS INFORMATION ✖ ABOUT A *STUDENT* TO IEP MEETINGS?

Of course, this is the responsibility of everyone on the team. Each person is on an IEP team because of a responsibility for the success of a unique student. It is each team member's responsibility to come to IEP meetings armed with personal experience and assessment data that help figure out how a student can work toward standards. How many of us have attended IEP meetings where people file in one by one, give a progress report on the student, and leave? There is no "team" effort at all. Sharing information about a student is as much a team process as developing the IEP, especially as a student begins working toward standards.

Families must be included as integral members of IEP teams. They bring a wealth of information that is critical to effective planning. Family members can share information about what has worked for their sons and daughters, family strengths and resources, incentives that schools cannot offer, and most important, their dreams of the future for their sons and daughters, along with challenges they are facing.

The students themselves should be involved in their own planning. Even students with significant disabilities can be challenged to determine their current skills, show how they learn best, and follow through with learning activities. It is not enough to have students simply attend their planning meetings; teachers and parents need to take an active role in preparing students for participation. Some students have had limited experience in expressing personal preferences and advocating for themselves. Speaking out about their preferences, particularly in the presence of authority figures, may be a new role for students, one for which they need guidance and feedback. Teachers and parents can help prepare students to participate in their planning meetings by talking about the meeting's purpose, describing what goes on and who typically attends, identifying the role each person will play in supporting a student's goals, and discussing issues before and after the meeting occurs.

Some students may benefit from rehearsing certain parts of the meeting, such as how to greet team members or ways to express preferences or suggest alternatives. Teachers can help prepare students for IEP planning on a daily basis by providing numerous opportunities to express choices and preferences. If a student requires accommodations, such as an augmentative communication device, arrangements need to be made before the meeting. The goal is for students to assume some control over their education with appropriate levels of support.

WHO DECIDES HOW STUDENTS CAN WORK TOWARD STANDARDS?

First of all, notice that this question is *not* "who decides *whether* a student will work toward standards." We are going to begin with the assumption that all students *will* work toward standards. Armed with information, it is now the job of the IEP team to figure out *how*. This planning takes the combined wisdom and expertise of every IEP team member, including the student. Special educators usually guide the process, keeping in mind the individual goals and needs of a student. General educators bring an understanding of the overall school program, with courses, activities, and events that could provide learning opportunities for a student. Administrators can pave the way to access to anything offered by the school and make it clear that each student has a right to this access. Parents, paraprofessionals, and other team members can suggest and provide opportunities for learning at home as well as in work and community settings. And a student can let the team know what he or she likes and does not like about the plan.

It may be helpful to write down who will follow through with each instructional activity so that it is clear, especially to those who may not be used to facilitating this type of instruction. The format in Form 3.1 may help organize this instruction.

WHO SUPPORTS STUDENTS IN THEIR WORK TOWARD STANDARDS?

Access to standards-based instruction gets students nowhere without the support they need to be successful. We have all heard horror stories over the years about "mainstreaming" being a fancy way of saying that students with disabilities were being dumped into general education classrooms and were failing miserably. Beyond access to environments that offer instruction toward standards, students need support to be successful. Here again is where the wisdom and expertise of every IEP team member is critical. Special educators organize the support, provide some of it themselves, provide some direct instruction themselves, and arrange time to work with paraprofessionals, related service providers, and general educators in developing accommodations and modifications that help students work toward standards. General educators can include students with even

Form 3.1. Organizing Partners to Provide Standards-Based Instruction and Assessment

Student			
Content Standard(s)			
Goal/Performance Indicator			
Instructor(s)	*Location(s)*	*Instructional Strategy(s)*	*Assessment Strategy(s)*

SOURCE: Adapted from the work of special educators in the state of Wyoming.

the most severe disabilities in their classroom instruction toward standards in many ways, with the help and support of special educators.

Community service providers, along with students and their families, have the responsibility to facilitate learning outside of school. Community service providers provide an important link to community resources and can assist students in learning to standards. For example, students can learn math and communication skills in work and other settings outside of the school building. What does this collaboration look like? A real-life example of one of the author's experiences with true community collaboration can be found in the following example.

Community Collaboration at Its Best

There is a professional, multiracial theater company in Minneapolis, Minnesota, called Mixed Blood. The theater got its name from its mission, to embrace Martin Luther King's dream. The company recently completed a production that included a cast of 8 children and 10 adults, representing at least that many races and cultures. My son had an opportunity to be part of that cast, and as I watched the show develop, I was particularly fascinated by the participation of a talented 12-year-old actor with multiple disabilities, among them a significant visual impairment. From the beginning, the director made it clear that this young actor was as much a part of the cast as everyone else and that, together, they would support her participation and success. One day, I stopped in to see how things were going and found the entire cast sitting in a circle on the floor with the director and choreographer, trying to figure out the choreography for this young actor within a very challenging scene. Everyone had ideas, and everyone helped the actor learn the steps as they took turns guiding her through the scene—over and over again for days, until they were satisfied that it worked just right and she was comfortable with all of the moves. The young actor was very shy at first and waited for people to tell her what to do and guide her into position. But the director encouraged her to speak for herself and to offer her own ideas as well.

Did including her take extra time? Yes, it took a lot of time. Was it worth it? I think that everyone in the cast would wonder why anyone would even ask whether it was worth it—she was as important to the production as any other actor or crew member—of any age or background—and the whole production would sink or swim based on their collective work.

Now for the hard questions—could this work in a classroom? Does education always need to take place in a classroom? Could this young actor be working toward standards in communication, performing arts, physical education, and social studies through her work with a theater company—instead of or in addition to work in a classroom? Can you see the doors that open with this single example? Just one example shows multiple standards, met in multiple settings, with all kinds of committed and collaborative support.

❖ WHO MAKES ALTERNATE ASSESSMENT PARTICIPATION DECISIONS?

By law, the decision to have a student participate in alternate assessments is to be made by that student's IEP team. The collective wisdom and expertise of all team members is needed to make a good decision. Everyone on the team needs to know about alternate assessments, their purpose, and how they are implemented. Everyone also needs to know about the consequences of alternate assessment participation for a student. For example, will the decision mean that the student is not eligible to graduate with a standard diploma because passing the general assessment is a graduation requirement? Chapter 4 discusses specific steps involved in making participation decisions. The team should go through these steps together, make an informed decision, and then document that decision on the IEP. Team members may differ in their opinion about participation. They should keep in mind that it is important to include a student in the general assessment with accommodations whenever possible and to reserve alternate assessment participation for students with the most significant cognitive impairments. Decisions should be made by consensus—not by a majority vote. It is possible that a person who disagrees with the rest of the group has important information to support his or her opinion. Disagreements about assessment decisions need to be addressed with the same seriousness using the same procedures as other disagreements.

To prepare families of students with disabilities and other IEP team members to make thoughtful and valid assessment participation decisions, they need information about state assessments and the participation options allowed within a state. Clear, brief, and timely written information is one strategy for preparing parents and other team members for this decision. Boxes 3.2 and 3.3 show examples of information contained in brochures for parents in two states. We will also tell you a story about the daughter of one of the authors (excerpts from Quenemoen & Quenemoen, 1999).

Parent to Parent: High Expectations, Assessment, and Accountability, but Most of All, Success

I am the mother of three successful young adults. They are in those wonderful but scary years of the "twenty somethings," and it is so gratifying to watch them find their way into their own lives. The oldest of the three, Alma, who likes to give tips to her two younger siblings on surviving roommates and juggling jobs and a social life, has Down syndrome. Alma lives with two other young women with similar interests, sharing a house that truly is theirs, with support services designed to help her be successful in her own life, not to run her life for her. She is also employed in a competitive, unsubsidized job of her choice. For Alma, the hard work she's done to build her own life is paying off.

Alma was born the month and year that Congress passed the law requiring a "free appropriate education" for children with disabilities, July of 1975. As part of a decade of efforts to ensure the civil rights of all people in the United States, P.L. 94-142 recognized the civil rights of children with disabilities to access to a public education. The elementary school principal in our small, rural school became our best ally in understanding how Alma would benefit from schooling—and he helped us and his staff understand that high expectations for Alma's success would lead to Alma's success!

I interviewed Alma a year ago for a newsletter article about her journey of high expectations. Her perspective is better than mine on how important those expectations were. She remembers her very early years of school. She said that getting help with things like speech, walking, and her balance when she was very young, along with learning to do things in school, helped her prepare for her life now. She remembers

Box 3.2

— *State 1: Information on the Statewide Assessment Program for Parents of Students With Disabilities*

The introduction begins with a belief statement—a great place to start!

"The belief that all students can learn is an underlying premise of our education reform legislation and policies. Accountability at the school, district, and state level must be based on educational results of all students. Student results are to be used as a basis for organizing instruction at the school and classroom level.

The requirement that students with disabilities participate in the statewide assessment program has created a great deal of interest and concern about the accommodations and/or modifications these students need in instruction and assessment to provide them with full and equal access to educational opportunities. This document is intended to provide information about how students with disabilities will participate in the Statewide Assessment Program."

This is followed by a question-and-answer section that includes the following questions:

- What is a statewide assessment?
- What is the Statewide Assessment Program?
- Who participates in the Statewide Assessment Program?
- Why should my child participate?
- Can I refuse to have my child participate?
- How will my child participate?
- What is the Alternate Assessment?
- Will students participating in the Alternate Assessment graduate with the same diploma as other students?
- How do I get more information about the participation of students with disabilities in the Alternate Assessment?

The guide concludes with participation criteria for the Alternate Assessment.

fondly the support she got from her teachers, classmates, and support staff during those early years. Getting ready for her life started long ago, in her mind.

There were high expectations, and she found she could meet those expectations. Here are some examples:

- In sixth grade, Alma gave a class presentation on Down syndrome while her health class was looking at their personal challenges and opportunities. It helped Alma begin taking over her own advocacy, and it led to open and supportive interactions with classmates who were just beginning to be keenly aware of "differences."

- The basic science she learned in junior high through hands-on science instruction helped her understand job-related issues, such as the use of chemicals in cleaning techniques, and life-related issues, such as reading the clouds to tell if a storm is coming.

Box 3.3

— *State 2: Questions and Answers About the Educational Assessment Program—Alternate Assessment—A Guide for Parents*

This guide is also set up in a question-and-answer format, with responses to the following questions:

- What is the Alternate Assessment?
- Who may participate in the Alternate Assessment?
- How often will my child be assessed with the Alternate Assessment?
- What does participation in the Alternate Assessment mean for my child?
- If my child's instruction occurs in the regular education classroom, may he/she participate in the Alternate Assessment?
- How will I learn the results of my child's performance?
- Who else will know my child's Alternate Assessment results?
- How will the results be reported?
- How can I help my child get ready for the Alternate Assessment?
- Whom do I contact if I have questions?

- When Alma's mathematics skills hit a plateau, she became frustrated with division tables that seemed too hard and too boring. But when she was able to figure out how much solution to make for cleaning tables at her part-time job, her math skills grew, and her frustration went away.

- When Alma worked in cooperative groups in senior high social studies class to figure out why there were wars in some parts of the world, she not only gained knowledge and an interest in world affairs, she cemented friendships she has to this day. One young woman classmate continues to write to Alma from Africa and the Middle East, where her work as a special education and English as a second language teacher has taken her.

When Alma talks about her success today, she mentions her teachers right away. "You know, some of them expected a lot of me, and sometimes that made me mad. When I wanted to watch the boys more than my paper in social studies class, my teacher got on my case. Now I know that's what I needed." Alma can tell you exactly which teachers were "good" and which weren't. For her, "good" means teachers who made an effort to understand how she learned and then worked with her to help her get everything she could out of the class. She says, "Feeling good about what I can do is important to me. Some teachers helped me with that, some didn't."

The Individuals with Disabilities Education Act (IDEA) is the "new" civil rights law for students with disabilities. Although these students received the right to attend schools over 25 years ago, the 1997 amendments to IDEA ensure that students with disabilities have access to the general education curriculum and that there are high expectations for each student to be successful. Although Alma went through school prior to these important amendments, we had a dedicated elementary school principal who laid down the law in his school about high expectations leading to success, and Alma's success is the result. He remained active on Alma's IEP team, and he made sure that we were all assessing her progress, figuring out ways to move her to the next level, and he held us all, including Alma, accountable for her achievement. With his encouragement, Alma was part of every IEP meeting from the time she was in first grade. Over time, she took over some leadership of the team meetings, and clearly, every team member felt accountable to and for her!

Every child with significant challenges to learning needs lots of support to move toward independence and success. High expectations, assessment, and accountability can be the tools we need to help each of our children succeed. Alternate assessment can give you and your child the opportunities for success that Alma and our family received through the leadership of a dedicated school principal. Take advantage of every opportunity, and you'll be able to help your child find success in a life that uniquely fits him or her. High expectations—combined with the tools of assessment and accountability—will lead to success (excerpts from Quenemoen & Quenemoen, 1999).

⊞ WHO CONDUCTS ALTERNATE ASSESSMENTS?

The people who conduct alternate assessments are the same people who support students in their instruction. There are several assessment strategies that can be used (described in Chapter 6), and each person assigned to collect data should be well versed in the strategies that they are expected to use. It is important that assessment be part of instruction and not separate from it, to elicit a student's best performance in situations that they are used to.

Parents are important collectors of alternate assessment data in home and community settings, using checklists and observations for documentation. It is important that everyone collecting assessment information understand exactly what they are to observe, as described in Chapter 6. Also, to increase the validity and reliability of the assessment, it is important to have more than one person assess students and in more than one setting.

This should ease the minds of special educators who thought they might have to run around with a clipboard all year, continually collecting data for alternate assessments as an add-on to their other million-and-one responsibilities. Assessment should be an ongoing process, a process as much a part of instruction as teaching. Just as special educators are responsible for arranging various aspects of a student's instruction, they are also usually in charge of compiling assessment data collected by all individuals involved in a student's instruction.

⊞ SUMMARY OF TASKS AND ROLES

As you think through each of the responsibilities involved in the implementation of standards and alternate assessments, you may find the worksheet in Table 3.1 helpful in identifying each person's role and responsibilities in the process. We have filled in the sample worksheet for you, followed by a blank form (Form 3.2) that you can customize for your situation. If you use this worksheet for an individual student, you could fill in specific names and responsibilities.

TABLE 3.1   Documentation of Tasks and Roles

General Task	Person	Specific Responsibility
Who brings information about standards and assessments to IEP teams?	All team members	Learn about standards and assessments through training and written information.
	General educators	Help other team members get up to speed about standards and assessments. Inform team members about training on standards that they could participate in together in the future.
	School administrators, counselors, and curriculum and assessment personnel	Bring important information about standards and assessments to IEP teams and set the expectation that each student will work toward standards.
Who brings information about a student to IEP meetings?	All team members	Bring information from the specific contexts in which they see a student.
	Families	Bring a wealth of information that is critical to effective planning.
Who decides how students can work toward standards?	Special educators	Organize instruction and support, lead IEP team in development of standards-based IEP.
	Related-service providers	Help develop accommodations and adaptations.
	Families	Assist team in selecting standards to work toward, advocate for participation in standards-based settings that help meet IEP goals.
Who provides instruction and supports students in their work toward standards?	General educators	Provide content area instruction in general education settings.
	Paraprofessionals	Support student learning in instructional settings.
	Families	Support student learning at home.
	Special educators and related-services providers	Work with partners to refine instructional strategies in various learning settings. Organize the support, provide some direct instruction, organize development and use of accommodations.
Who makes alternate assessment participation decisions?	All team members	The collective wisdom and expertise of all team members is needed to make participation decisions.
Who conducts alternate assessments?	Special educators	Organize the alternate assessment data collection process and conduct some assessments.
	All team members— including families	Conduct assessment and collect data.

Form 3.2.   Documentation of Tasks and Roles

General Task	Person	Specific Responsibility
Who brings information about standards and assessments to IEP teams?		
Who brings information about a student to IEP meetings?		
Who decides how students can work toward standards?		
Who provides instruction and supports students in their work toward standards?		
Who makes alternate assessment participation decisions?		
Who conducts alternate assessments?		

✖ ON A LARGER SCALE—WHO DEVELOPS ALTERNATE ASSESSMENT SYSTEMS IN THE FIRST PLACE?

Many states have involved groups of people (i.e., stakeholder groups, task forces, advisory groups) in the development of their alternate assessment systems. The National Center on Educational Outcomes (NCEO) collected information about these groups and their responsibilities. Box 3.4 contains examples of stakeholders from seven states (Thompson & Thurlow, 2000). See Box 3.5 for some excellent sources of information about collaboration.

Box 3.4

Examples of Stakeholders in the Development of State-Level Alternate Assessments

State 1 identified stakeholders through a variety of sources: local directors of special education and assessment, the Institutions of Higher Education Forum, the State Special Education Advisory Committee, the state Parent Center, and other interested individuals. The state also surveyed colleagues with content area curriculum and instruction expertise for task force participants in each content area.

State 2 has an Alternate Assessment Task Force that is representative of the state's geographical regions and includes parents, school, and state personnel who represent a variety of positions, including special education teachers, administrators, testing coordinators, curriculum directors, and higher education representatives. Some roles overlap (e.g., three members were actually parents of students with disabilities, although only one represented that perspective alone). An expanded work group, including several teachers of students with significant needs, completed the process.

State 3 has two committees working on various components of the alternate assessment and extended standards. The committees contain special education teachers, parents, general education administrators, special school staff, school psychologists, a technology consultant, and curriculum adaptations specialists. University personnel are developing the Alternate Assessment.

State 4 has an advisory board consisting of teachers (regular and special), university personnel, parents, and state department representatives. This group meets for 3 days every summer and once during the school year to discuss refinements and revisions.

State 5 has standards that were chosen by an expert panel and reviewed for content validity. The advisory committee has been meeting on an annual basis to review procedures and results as well as to make necessary adjustments as appropriate. Parents, advocates, school personnel, test personnel, and others are included on the advisory committee.

State 6 has an Alternate Assessment Committee that represents elementary, middle, and secondary teachers of students with significant disabilities and parents and college faculty from nine regions across the state. The participants agreed, as part of this experience, to return to their regions and conduct a meeting to share the results of the initial meeting with other teachers, local district administrators, and parents. Over 500 additional stakeholders participated in nine regional meetings and provided structured feedback. The Alternate Assessment Committee then reviewed input from the regional meetings.

State 7 has a group of "Key Informants" (special educators, general educators, parents, administrators, university personnel, and Department of Public Instruction representatives) who were brought together to review issues related to the creation of the alternate assessment and to prepare written recommendations about this aspect of accountability for results of the education process. Writing teams were assembled (general educators—content area and special educators) to review the content standards and identify how the content standards and benchmarks could be expanded to address the needs of all students.

Box 3.5

▬ *Resources—The "Wheel" Has Already Been Invented!*

There are many excellent sources of information about the ways in which partners can collaborate in the successful participation of students with disabilities in the general curriculum. Standards have not been reflected in many of these resources to date, but strategies for inclusive education reflect over 20 years of research and practice. Here are some examples and ideas:

Check out the journals from professional organizations, such as the Council for Exceptional Children's journal, *Teaching Exceptional Children.* For example, the Fall 1998 issue of this journal is devoted entirely to the topic of inclusive schools and schoolwide achievement. Several articles in that issue are especially relevant to this chapter, including "Promoting Successful Inclusion Through Collaborative Problem-Solving," by Tim Hobbs and David L. Westling. These authors make the important point that "Serving students with disabilities in inclusive settings depends greatly on effective collaboration among professionals" (p. 15). The authors describe a typical problem-solving process, but the real gem in this article is the example of a team process around an individual student, 10-year-old Jason. Jason had several difficulties participating in general education classes, and his team increased his success by identifying problems and making plans in the context of a structured team process; including everyone affected by the problem, including teachers, parents, and the student; dealing with problems in an ongoing manner; documenting problems and solution activities; keeping the planning and solution process flexible; rewarding positive results and celebrating successes; and carrying out planning and solutions in a truly collaborative environment.

Another article in the Fall 1998 issue of *Teaching Exceptional Children* is called "Using the 'Write Talk-Nology' with Patrik," by Karen A. Erickson and David A. Koppenhaver. This article demonstrates how an 11-year-old student with multiple disabilities worked on reading, writing, and communication skills in a 4th-grade general education setting by communicating with a DynaVox Communication Device.

One more article in this issue deserves mention here: "In Junior High You Take Earth Science: Including a Student with Severe Disabilities into an Academic Class," by Ellin Siegel-Causey, Carol McMorris, Susan McGowen, and Sue Sands-Buss. This article discusses strategies for including a 14-year-old student with multiple disabilities in a general education 8th-grade science class. The need for high standards is implied by Cory's mom who wanted her son to "get more out of (these classes) than learning how to sit and be a good boy" (p. 66). The partners in Cory's education found they needed to determine educator roles, duties, and communication strategies; establish curriculum adaptations and level of student participation; and monitor progress and revise teaching strategies to ensure his success.

Another great professional organization to use as a resource when you are trying to figure out how to support students with severe disabilities in their work toward standards is the *Association for Persons with Severe Disabilities.* This organization has a journal that provides practical research-based models for collaborative support in nearly every issue.

4

Assessment
Participation Decisions

TOUGH QUESTIONS

Who decides which students should participate in alternate assessments?

Should most students with disabilities participate in large-scale assessments?

Are some students too low functioning to participate in alternate assessments?

I have a student who does very poorly on state tests even though I think he can read most of the questions. He hardly ever finishes and has a hard time finding the right place to fill in the bubbles on the answer sheet. Should he participate in alternate assessments?

We began the first chapter with the statement, "All children can learn." Then, we talked about how all children could learn toward high standards and who should be involved. The next question, of course, is "How do we know that all children have made progress toward high standards?" It makes sense that if we know that all children can learn, we should be able to figure out what and how well each child is learning. But just as children don't all learn in the same way, they also cannot all be assessed in the same way. Alternate assessments give us other ways to assess student learning. They help us to determine not "whether" students can learn or "whether" that learning can be assessed but "how" students learn best and "how" they can best be assessed. How do we decide how to best assess a student? Who should participate in general assessments, possibly with accommodations, and who are the best candidates for participation in alternate assessments? This chapter offers insights and tools to help make these decisions.

How Should Lara Participate?

Last year, Lara's state mandated that all 8th graders would be included in the state assessment and accountability system. Because Lara was in 8th grade, a decision about her participation had to be made. She could either participate in the general assessment with accommodations, or she could be included as an alternate assessment participant. Exemption was no longer an option.

At first, Lara's IEP team members were frustrated with the "no exemption" policy. Even though an "all students" directive had been given, many said, "But that can't be for Lara." They expressed feelings like, "Lara can't participate in the alternate assessment. It will make her too tired and uncomfortable" and "This is too hard—we shouldn't ask so much of Lara." But state officials persisted with, "Lara is an 8th grader, she's in your school, she will be assessed, and she will be counted." That opened the door to asking "how" and "what."

Once the special education staff understood that what Lara knew and could do was to be measured through an alternate assessment, a connection had to be made with the school counselor, the person who arranged the assessments. Unfortunately, he had already marked Lara as "exempt" on the assessment participation list. As in the past, a decision had been made that she was not to be included on any list that was used for assessment or accountability. The teachers convinced the counselor to document Lara's participation in the alternate assessment.

What About Mark?

Mark is a 10th-grade student. Mark has autism and exhibits very poor fine motor skills, little social language, and echolalia. At first, his IEP team assumed that he should participate in alternate assessments. In fact, his special education teacher didn't really give it a second thought.

But Mark has some skills that need to be considered. For example, he can read just about anything. He can tell a scribe what he wants written down. He can look up information in a book. He can read a passage and answer questions about facts found in the passage to a scribe, who fills in the bubbles on the answer page. He responds to "what" questions easily but has trouble with "why." He watches "Who Wants to Be a Millionaire?" on TV and can answer many of the questions correctly.

With this information, does it sound like Mark should participate in an alternate assessment or in a general assessment with accommodations? The special education staff saw him as a student with autism who was working on basic communication and math skills—a few years below grade level. The principal, who knew how much time Mark spent in general education classes and how well he could use a computer, thought he should participate in the general assessment with accommodations.

The special education staff argued that other 10th graders were not working on following two-step directions. They were working on writing essays—Mark was working on simple sentences. There were several classes he couldn't take because he can't stand noise (like welding). Mark's state has a rule that all students must be certified in CPR (cardiopulmonary resuscitation) to graduate with a regular diploma. Mark is so tactilely defensive, the teachers could not even get him to touch the training mannequin. If he can't even graduate with a diploma, why should he bother taking the general assessment?

Participation decisions for students like Mark cannot be made based on his label. The fact that he has autism does not determine how he will participate in the assessment. Making assessment participation decisions for Mark forced the special education staff to honestly question whether they were holding high enough expectations for him. They realized that the team had to be much broader than just special educators. They found that sometimes they were too protective and too close to students like Mark to make decisions based on high enough expectations.

Though frustrating, it was OK for Mark's IEP team to have some doubts as it struggled with assessment participation decisions. Team members realized that they could not make decisions without really considering Mark's uniqueness and complexity. The team also knew that its decision would need to be reconsidered every testing year.

WHAT THE LAWS SAY

There are two primary laws that talk about participation in alternate assessments. These are, of course, the 1997 amendments to the Individuals with Disabilities Education Act, and Title I of the Improving America's Schools Act of 1994. The exact citations from these laws are found in Box 4.1 (IDEA) and Box 4.2 (IASA).

ASSESSMENT PARTICIPATION OPTIONS

There are generally three options for assessment participation. These are (a) participation in general assessments without accommodations, (b) participation in general assessments with accommodations, and (c) participation in alternate assessments. Some states have additional options, such as participation in some type of modified test. Other states allow some students to take tests designed for students at lower grade levels. This practice is generally known as "out-of-level" testing and has become quite controversial.

Percentages are often given to show approximately how many students are expected to participate in different ways. For example, about 85% of students with disabilities have relatively mild or moderate disabilities and can participate in state and national large-scale assessments, either with or without accommodations (Ysseldyke, Thurlow, McGrew, & Shriner, 1994). These percentages are useful, not to provide caps or cutoff points but to give people an idea about the rates they might expect. Decision makers start from the premise that students are to participate, to the extent possible, in general assessments rather than in alternate assessments.

Box 4.1

━ *Amendments to the Individuals with Disabilities Education Act, P.L. 105-17 (1997)*

"As appropriate, the State or local educational agency develops guidelines for the participation of children with disabilities in alternate assessments for those children who cannot participate in State and districtwide assessment programs." (Sec. 612(a)(18)(A)(i))

━ *IDEA: Questions and Answers About Provisions in the Individuals with Disabilities Education Act Amendments of 1997 Related to Students with Disabilities and State and Districtwide Assessments (August 24, 2000)*

"The IEP team determines HOW individual students with disabilities participate in assessment programs, NOT WHETHER. The only students with disabilities who are exempted from participation in general State and districtwide assessment programs are students with disabilities convicted as adults under State law and incarcerated in adult prisons (34 CFR §300.311(b)(1)). With this statutory exception, there should be no language in State or district assessment guidelines, rules, or regulations that permits IEP teams to exempt students from State or districtwide assessment programs.

Inclusion in assessments provides valuable information that benefits students either by indicating individual progress against standards or in evaluating educational programs. In some States, participation in assessments is a means to access benefits such as promotion and graduation. Given these benefits, exclusion from assessment programs based on disability would potentially violate Section 504 and Title II of the ADA."

There may be confusion when using percentages about whether they include the percentage of all students at a particular grade level or the percentage of students with disabilities. In Table 4.1, for example, the percentage of all students at a grade level expected to participate in alternate assessments is approximately .5% to 2%, whereas the percentage of students *with disabilities* expected to participate is 5% to 20%. A large percentage of students with disabilities is expected to participate in general assessments with the use of accommodations (30%-70%). These ranges in percentages are wide for several reasons. States have different types of assessments and different assessment systems. States also allow different accommodations for different assessments, some of which may be used by any student with a need and some of which may only be used by students with disabilities. In some places, the use of accommodations is encouraged, and in other places, accommodations are discouraged. Often, the more effective the use of accommodations, the more students are likely to participate in general, rather than alternate, assessments.

✣ ASSESSMENT ACCOMMODATIONS

One of the ways to ensure the inclusion of many students with disabilities in assessments is by providing them with testing accommodations. Accommodations are simply alterations in the way a test is administered, without changing the actual test content or performance standard. An assessment accommodation is provided because of a student need, not to give students with disabilities an advantage. When students with disabilities

Box 4.2

━ *Elementary & Secondary Education Act as Amended by the Improving America's Schools Act of 1994, P.L. 103-382 (1994)*

"High-quality, yearly student assessments . . . will be used as the primary means of determining the yearly performance of each local educational agency and school served under this part in enabling all children served under this part to meet the State's student performance standards. Such assessments shall be the same assessments used to measure the performance of all children, if the State measures the performance of all children [and will] . . . provide for the participation in such assessments of all students." (Sec. 1111(b)(3)(A))

━ *Letter and Attachment (Summary Guidance on the Inclusion Requirement for Title I Final Assessments) From Assistant Secretary for Elementary and Secondary Education Mike Cohen (April 7, 2000)*

"Individualized education program (IEP) teams or Section 504 placement teams are responsible for determining whether a student is able to participate in the standard assessment, and if so, what (if any) accommodations are appropriate. The State's obligation is to provide reasonable accommodations necessary to validly measure the achievement of students with disabilities relative to State standards. In those infrequent cases when an IEP team or Section 504 team determines that standard assessments, even with reasonable accommodations, do not provide a student with an opportunity to demonstrate her or his knowledge and skills, then the State or school district must provide an alternate assessment." (Attachment on Summary Guidance, p. 2)

TABLE 4.1	Three Kinds of Assessment Participation for Students With Disabilities: Estimated Participation Rates

Type of Participation	Percentage of All Students at the Grade Level Assessed	Percentage of Students With Disabilities at the Grade Level Assessed
General assessment	80-95	40-75
General assessment with accommodations	3-7	30-70
Alternate assessment	.5-2	5-20

SOURCE: From Ysseldyke, Thurlow, McGrew, & Shriner (1994).

use assessment accommodations, it is to show what they know without being impeded by their disabilities. Accommodations offset the impact of a disability and are legally required under Section 504 of the Rehabilitation Act (and reflected in 504 accommodation plans) and the Americans with Disabilities Act.

Accommodations can be categorized into at least six types: setting, presentation, timing, response, scheduling, and other. The "other" category catches any accommoda-

John E. Riley Library
Northwest Nazarene University

tions that a student may need that do not fit into the other five areas. A brief description of each of these categories follows. Examples of accommodations and decision-making questions can be found in Table 4.2

1. *Setting accommodations* change the location in which an assessment is given or the conditions of the assessment setting. For example, a student who has difficulty focusing attention in a group setting or needs to take frequent breaks may be assessed in a different room, either individually or with a small group. A student who uses special equipment, such as a tape recorder, may also need an individualized setting. Changes in settings could include special lighting, acoustics, or furniture.

2. *Timing accommodations* change the allowable length of testing time and may also change the way that time is organized. This is the type of accommodation requested most often by students who need extra time to process written text, extra time to write, or time to use certain equipment. Some students may also need frequent or extended breaks.

3. *Scheduling accommodations* change the particular time of day, day of the week, or number of days over which a test is administered. These changes may be made based on a student's medication or ability to stay alert for the test.

4. *Presentation accommodations* change the way in which an assessment is given to a student and include format alterations, procedural changes, and use of assistive devices. Presentation accommodations tend to be the most controversial, especially in the area of reading tests to students.

5. *Response accommodations* change how a student responds to an assessment. As with presentation accommodations, these changes may be in the form of format alterations (e.g., marking responses in the test booklet rather than on a separate page), procedural changes (e.g., giving a response in a different mode, such as pointing, oral response, or sign language), and the use of assistive devices (e.g., scribe writes student responses, brailler, calculator, communication device). Some of these accommodations are also very controversial.

6. *Other accommodations* include out-of-level testing, which means taking a test at a lower grade level. For example, an 8th grader who is functioning below grade level takes a 4th grade test rather than the test typically given to 8th graders. Out-of-level testing is highly controversial and not recommended unless tests across grades can be scored on the same scale. Another accommodation that does not fit into any of the foregoing categories is motivational: encouraging students to finish a test and do their best.

⌗ PARTICIPATION DECISION MAKERS

The IEP team must determine whether a student with disabilities receiving special education services will participate in assessments under standardized conditions, with or without accommodations, or will participate in alternate assessments. The laws and guidance quoted earlier state that the responsibility for assessment participation decisions rests squarely on the shoulders of a student's IEP team. This is an important re-

TABLE 4.2   Examples of Accommodations and Decision-Making Questions

Setting	Presentation
Examples	*Examples*
Administer the test in a small group or individually in a separate location with minimal distractions.	Provide test on audiotape.
	Increase spacing between items or reduce items per page or line.
Provide special lighting.	Highlight key words or phrases in directions.
Provide special furniture or acoustics.	Provide cues (e.g., arrows and stop signs) on answer form.
Questions	*Questions*
Can the student focus on his or her own work in a room with other students?	Can the student listen and follow oral directions?
Does the student display behaviors that are distracting to other students?	Can the student see and hear?
Can the student take a test in the same way as it is administered to other students?	Can the student read?

Timing	Response
Examples	*Examples*
Allow a flexible schedule.	Allow marking of answers in booklet.
Extend the time allotted to take the test.	Tape-record responses for later translation.
Allow frequent breaks during testing.	Allow use of scribe.
	Provide copying assistance between drafts.
Questions	*Questions*
Can the student work continuously for the entire length of a typically administered portion of the test (e.g., 20 to 30 minutes)?	Can the student track from a test booklet to a test response form?
Does the student use accommodations that require more time to complete test items?	Is the student able to manipulate a pencil or other writing instrument?

Scheduling	Other
Examples	*Examples*
Administer the test in several sessions, possibly over several days, specifying the duration of each session.	Special test preparation
	On-task or focusing prompts
Allow subtests to be taken in a different order.	Any accommodation that a student needs that does not fit under the existing categories
Administer the test at different times of day.	
Questions	*Questions*
Does the student take medication that dissipates over time, with optimal performance at a certain time of day?	Is this the first time that the student will be taking a district or state assessment?
Does the student's anxiety level increase dramatically when working in certain content areas so that these should be aministered after other content areas?	Does the student have the necessary test-taking skills?

SOURCE: From Elliott, Ysseldyke, Thurlow, and Erickson (1997).

sponsibility and involves more than just a simple check on an IEP form. All IEP team members need to be clear about the fact that they are not to consider *whether* a student will participate in assessments but *how* that participation might take place. They should also work under the assumption that most students should participate in general assessments, with accommodations as needed, and that only a small percentage of students will participate in alternate assessments. Each IEP team member needs enough information about assessment participation options to be able to make informed decisions with a student. An in-depth discussion of the roles and responsibilities of each partner was addressed in Chapter 3.

For making participation decisions, several state assessment guidelines suggest that IEP teams begin with the following premises:

- The decision about a student's participation in state and districtwide assessments is an IEP team decision and not an administrative decision.
- Decisions are made at the IEP meeting that precedes the administration of any state or districtwide assessment.
- Participation decisions are reviewed annually.

✖ PARTICIPATION DECISION-MAKING PROCESS

When an IEP team meets to decide how a student should participate in assessments, they might begin by reviewing a list of things that the decision *should not* be based on. The following list (or some variation) is found in the participation guidelines of several states. Remember, these are *not* reasons for a student to be in an alternate assessment.

- Academically behind due to excessive absences, poor attendance, or lack of instruction
- Unable to complete the general academic curriculum because of social, cultural, or economic differences
- Disability category, educational placement, type of instruction, amount of time receiving special education services, or some combination of these
- The student's IQ
- Disruptive behavior
- Below-average reading level
- Expectations of poor performance
- Low achievement in general

Currently, some guidelines state that students who are not working toward district or state standards should not participate in general district or state assessments—and are likely candidates for alternate assessments. As we learn more about how all students can work toward the same standards, participation decisions will no longer be based on such statements as these: "Student is not working toward state standards" or "Student has a different curriculum."

As discussed in Chapter 2, we believe that every student has a right to and can work toward high educational standards. Students may be showing what they have learned in different ways, and they may be working on different skills at different levels of compe-

---

Box 4.3

━ *Final Regulations for the Amendments to the Individuals with Disabilities Education Act, P.L. 105-17 (1997)*

"The IDEA Amendments of 1997 require that all children with disabilities be included in general State and districtwide assessment programs, with appropriate accommodations, where necessary. In some cases, alternate assessments may be necessary, depending on the needs of the child, and not the category or severity of the child's disability." (Content of IEP, Discussion, p. 12593-12594)

Box 4.4

━ *Guidance on Standards, Assessments, and Accountability That Supplements the Elementary and Secondary Education Act as Amended by the Improving America's Schools Act of 1994, P.L. 103-382 (1997)*

"What does it mean to say that standards apply to all children? Whether standards apply statewide or districtwide, all students within that State or district must be held to the same challenging standards. In other words, all students, including . . . students with diverse learning needs, are expected to learn the same general high-quality content, rather than a separate curriculum for certain students, although a wide range of instructional methods and strategies could be used. All students are held to the same high standards of performance, regardless of the assessment instrument used. Students can and will vary in their performance levels—some students will learn more than others. However, the performance levels all students need to reach in order to 'meet the standard' will be set much higher than at present." (I. Content and Performance Standards, Questions #12, p. 7 of 8)

---

tence, but the standards should stand out as the beacon toward which all students progress (see Box 4.3 and Box 4.4).

Consider this standard: "Students will develop and apply the communication skills of listening, speaking, and viewing through a variety of informal and formal opportunities." Is there any student who should not be working toward that standard? Granted, standards in some states and districts are more specific and are identified for specific grade levels. These may need to be expanded to be as inclusive as the standard cited above. The point here is that participation decisions cannot be based on whether a student is working toward standards, because *all* students can and should be working toward standards.

So far, we have talked about what assessment participation decisions *should not* be based on. It's about time we discuss what those decisions *should* be based on. Using common sense, if we are talking about an alternate assessment, we should be thinking about students who need an alternate way of showing what they know and can do—an alternate to a written test. The deciding factor, then, is the need for an alternate way of showing what they know and can do. The question IEP teams need to ask is "Can this student show what he or she knows on paper-and-pencil tests, even with accommodations?" If the answer is no, even with the accommodations the student is accustomed to using in daily instruction, then participation in alternate assessments would be a likely choice. Notice that the question is not "Can the student do well on the test?" There are students who may not perform well, even with accommodations that they are accustomed to using. When this concern arises (and it will), we need to go back to the purpose of the test. The purpose of this type of assessment, as described back in the first chapter, is to see how all of the students at a particular grade level are progressing toward standards. It is important to see who is doing well and who is not, so that programmatic and budgetary adjustments can be made.

The bottom line is that if a student can participate in the general assessment with accommodations but a low score is anticipated, that student should still participate in the general assessment with accommodations. In addition, nearly all students should be working toward grade-level benchmarks within the standards, using carefully selected accommodations as needed. The first question to ask about students who are not working on benchmarks is "Why not?" Are the expectations too low? Does the student need accommodations that are not available for some reason? Is a special education teacher who is not certified in a content area (for example, high school math) teaching the student watered-down content in a special education resource room? Is the student lost in a general education classroom without the support needed to learn high-level content? With higher expectations, authentic instruction, increased test-taking skills, effective use of accommodations, and incentives for greater assessment participation, most students can participate in general assessments.

Reserve alternate assessment participation for the few students who cannot participate in general assessments, no matter what accommodations are provided. These are students who cannot respond to any test items and can only show that they have made progress toward standards through participation in alternate assessments. Figure 4.1 shows a practical assessment participation decision process.

Lara is one of a very small number of students who are working toward standards in a different way. For example, Lara is learning to look at a book and hit a large switch when a particular icon appears. As an 8th grader, this is a much different skill than one of the 8th-grade benchmarks in her state, for example, "Apply literal and inferential comprehension strategies to analyze a variety of genres from diverse cultures and time periods." Is Lara working toward a reading standard? *Yes!* Can she show what she knows and can do on the 8th-grade general assessment? No. Does she need to show what she knows and can do toward the reading standard in a different way? Yes. Lara is a likely candidate for alternate assessment participation.

What about Mark, the student described earlier in this chapter? Mark is working toward high standards with appropriate accommodations. His IEP team now believes that he can probably show what he knows on the general assessment. Becca, the 9-year-old 4th grader with Down syndrome we met back in Chapter 1, is another student who may be able to participate in general assessments with the accommodations she is accustomed to using.

✛ DOCUMENTING PARTICIPATION DECISIONS ON THE IEP

IEP teams should make assessment participation decisions based on a process like the one shown in Figure 4.1. IEP forms are often made up of simple checklists for efficiency,

Figure 4.1. Participation Decision-Making Process

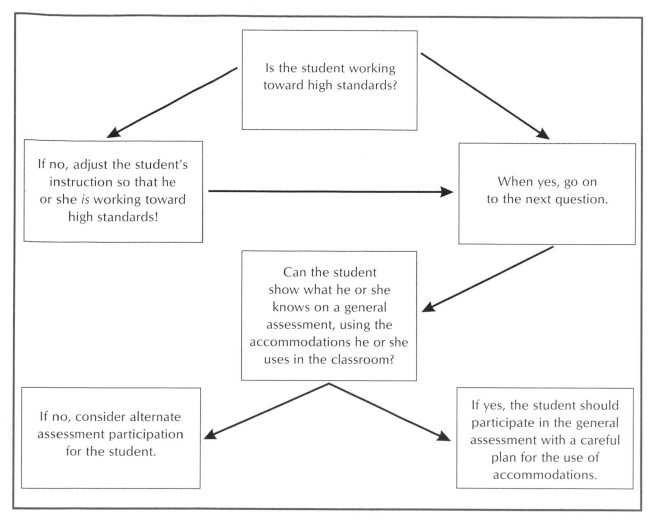

and it is easy to just check a box without carefully making a team decision and thinking through the implications of that decision. Details of IEP documentation are discussed in Chapter 5.

EXAMPLES OF ALTERNATE ASSESSMENT PARTICIPANTS

We have already described Lara, a student who might be selected to participate in alternate assessments, and Mark, a student who may be able to participate in general assessments with accommodations. Here follow descriptions of other students who are likely alternate-assessment participants. These examples are offered to show that we really are talking about a very small number of students, those with the most significant disabilities who cannot show what they know and can do on general assessments, even with accommodations.

ways: standard participation, participation with accommodations, or participation in alternate assessments."

- Address the use of "nonstandard" accommodations or "modifications" in state guidelines—with alternatives for students who can participate successfully in standard assessments with accommodations that they are accustomed to using in the classroom but are considered nonstandard on the assessment.

- Hold serious discussions with test developers about making test items accessible to a broader range of students and increasing the range of test item difficulty to give more information about higher- and lower-performing students (consider the use of computer-adapted tests, some of which can test students across a broad span of age and ability without overwhelming students with too many items).

As districts and states become more accustomed to inclusive standards and assessment, guidelines will be refined and improved. It is important to stay up-to-date on the accommodations allowed for each district or statewide assessment. Many states post current assessment information on their education agency's Web site. Once again, links to state Web sites are available through CCSSO at http://www.ccsso.org/seamenu.html.

5

Standards-Based IEPs, Transition Plans, and Alternate Assessments

TOUGH QUESTIONS

Do students with "maintenance only" IEPs need to address standards?

How will alternate assessments be correlated with the IEP?

What do we do if our state's IEP form does not mention standards or alternate assessments?

Is it possible to address standards and transition on the same IEP?

For a few years after the individualized education program came into being in 1975, there was a flurry of activity, including research, training, and development of models and strategies, as people figured out what an IEP was and how it should be written. There was a tremendous focus in both preservice and inservice training on eligibility determination, correct verbiage for goals and objectives, and overall compliance with the new law. Now, more than 25 years later, IEP teams have a new responsibility, one that extends far beyond the process of proper IEP development. There is an increased emphasis on access to the general education curriculum; teams now need to focus on high standards, on what students are actually learning as a result of their "special" programs and services, and on what needs to be done to prepare students for a meaningful transition to adult life.

IEPs developed with standards in mind (we'll call these "standards-based IEPs") can offer students a broader range of educational opportunities than they have ever had before. Standards-based IEPs can also provide the information needed to complete alternate assessments. To give alternate assessment participants an opportunity to work toward standards, even at the most basic or functional levels, standards must be addressed on their IEPs.

Focusing on standards sheds new light on the entire planning process engaged in by IEP teams. In the past, teams would assess a student's academic and functional skills, document problems and deficiencies on a form as a student's present level of educational performance, and then write goals and objectives to help a student overcome these deficits. For example, in a study about IEPs, Giangreco, Dennis, Edelman, and Cloninger (1994) found these goals:

Student will

- "Improve visual cognitive attention to a task following brief engagements of vestibular stimulation."
- "Initiate correction to mid-line when displaced laterally while prone or sitting astride horse or bolster."

With standards, the process changes. Now, rather than focusing on a student's deficits, we have an opportunity to focus on helping them work toward standards. Now, instead of making a long list of "What's wrong with this child?" We can start with "What are we working toward? How far along is this child now? What can we do to help the child move closer to meeting the standard?" And for students making the important transition from school to adult life, we can ask, "How will this standard help this student prepare for a successful transition from school to adult life?"

This chapter introduces you to a process for developing standards-based IEPs for alternate assessment participants as they progress through school and prepare for their transition to adult life. We hope that after reading this chapter, you will see how useful standards-based goals can be in a student's life. We have an opportunity to place those goals in real-life contexts as stepping stones toward standards that students and everyone who supports them can be accountable for.

Could Lara's IEP Be Standards-Based?

After learning about standards and how they could include students like Lara, her IEP team found that it did not know which skills or performance indicators to work on to show progress toward standards. The team would select

Box 5.1

—*Final Regulations for the Amendments to the Individuals with Disabilities Education Act, P.L. 105-17 (1999)*

Purpose of Special Education is ". . . to ensure access of the child to the general curriculum, so that he or she can meet the educational standards within the jurisdiction of the public agency that apply to all children." (34 CFR §300.2.6(b)(3)(i))

something, and Lara's mom would say, "Why that one?" The team soon admitted that it needed more information. Team members realized that the "present level of educational performance" they had written on Lara's IEP was not adequate for designing a standards-based education program, so they went back to the drawing board.

Lara's "present levels of educational performance" in the past had only dealt with physical needs—for feeding, range of motion, personal hygiene, and other activities that were done to Lara to pass the day and keep her healthy. For the first time, Lara would be assessed on what she knew and could do. The team chose COACH (*Choosing Outcomes and Accommodations for Children* [Giangreco, Cloninger, & Iverson, 1998]). The team asked a few general education teachers and Lara's mom to do it with them. Team members learned that Lara's mom was not even really sure about what Lara could do, because the school had been taking care of her for so long. As a team, they identified about five things from the assessment that were priorities for Lara and could be worked on to show progress toward standards.

Now, Lara's IEP team had data and could actually propose standards, goals, and objectives based on something, and it went smoothly because they had some direction to work toward. This was a big change from traditional IEP meetings that consisted mainly of reports from each staff person, resulting in IEPs that did not look much different from one year to the next.

WHAT THE LAWS SAY ⌗

IDEA 97 talks about the access of students with disabilities to the general curriculum. As you read in Chapter 2, standards provide the framework for the general curriculum across every state in this country. Therefore, if students with disabilities have access to the general curriculum, they will be working toward the same high standards as students who do not receive special education services. The importance of this access is stated in IDEA 97, as part of the purpose of special education (see Box 5.1).

This is an important point, because IDEA does not specifically include standards in IEPs. It is implied in requirements to ensure access to the general curriculum. Though IDEA does not address standards-based IEPs directly, the regulations do address the important participation of students with disabilities in the general curriculum (see Box 5.2).

Similarly, though participation in alternate assessments is addressed in IDEA, it is only implied under how a child will be assessed. Unfortunately, in state efforts to

Box 5.2

— *Final Regulations for the Amendments to the Individuals with Disabilities Education Act, P.L. 105-17 (1999)*

"The IEP for each child with a disability must include a statement of:
- the child's present levels of educational performance, including how the child's disability affects the child's involvement and progress in the general curriculum (i.e., the same curriculum as for nondisabled children)
- measurable annual goals, including benchmarks or short-term objectives, related to meeting the child's needs that result from the child's disability to enable the child to be involved in and progress in the general curriculum (i.e., the same curriculum as for nondisabled children), and meeting each of the child's other educational needs that result from the child's disability." (34 CFR §300.347(a)(1)(2))

Box 5.3

— *Final Regulations for the Amendments to the Individuals with Disabilities Education Act, P.L. 105-17 (1999)*

"The IEP for each child with a disability must include a statement of:
Any individual modifications in the administration of State or districtwide assessments of student achievement that are needed for the child to participate in the assessment; and
   (ii) If the IEP team determines that the child will not participate in a particular State or districtwide assessment of student achievement (or part of an assessment) a statement of
      (A) Why that assessment is not appropriate for the child; and
      (B) How the child will be assessed. (34 CFR §300.347(a)(1)(2))

streamline IEP forms and reduce paperwork, state IEP forms often contain only specific items from the law—and do not specifically address either standards or alternate assessments. This becomes a problem when IEP teams, who may not have anything in front of them but the state form, do not understand that both standards and alternate assessments are implied within the form but are not clearly stated (see Box 5.3).

Documenting assessment participation on IEP forms varies from state to state. Box 5.4 shows an excerpt from a state's IEP form that allows IEP teams to check how a student will participate in assessments. This form would be easy for a team that was familiar with the decision-making process described in Chapter 4 to complete. It would be very difficult for a team that did not have good information about participation options.

Some state IEP forms are less clear. That is why it is so important to make assessment participation decisions as a team and then find a way to document the decision on the form, rather than to use the form to make a decision. Box 5.5 shows an example of this type of form.

Box 5.4

— *Excerpt From a State IEP Form That Clearly States Participation Options*

___ Student participates in regular testing conditions with no accommodations.
___ Student participates with accommodations as documented on the attached Checklist.
___ Student participates in the Alternate Assessment. The Eligibility Guidelines form is attached.

Box 5.5

— *Excerpt From a State IEP Form That Only Implies Alternate Assessment Participation*

___ Yes, the student will participate and no adaptations (accommodations or modifications) are needed.
___ Yes, the student will participate with adaptations (accommodations or modifications) as listed in the Program Adaptations Section.
___ No, the student will not participate. Explain why each assessment is not appropriate. How will the student be assessed?

HOW TO BUILD A STANDARDS-BASED IEP ✕

There are several important steps in the effective and efficient development of standards-based IEPs. The steps are listed in Table 5.1, with instructions for completing each step below.

Step 1: Learn about district and state standards.

This step was covered back in Chapter 2 but bears mentioning again. It is impossible to develop a standards-based IEP without becoming intimately familiar with state and district standards across all content or learning areas—not just those currently assessed by state or district tests. If IEP teams are going to address standards on a student's IEP, they need to be familiar with the standards. Often, special educators have been excluded from discussions about standards and, thinking standards had nothing to do with them, did not take the time to become familiar with them. Use the checklist in Table 5.2 to test IEP team knowledge about state and district standards.

Step 2: Find out what has been done to include all students in district and state standards.

This step was also covered in Chapter 2 and needs to be emphasized again in the development of standards-based IEPs. Some states have done extensive work with many stakeholders at the state and local levels on making connections between the skills

TABLE 5.1	**Instructions for Building a Standards-Based IEP**

❑ Step 1: Learn about district and state standards.

❑ Step 2: Find out what has been done to include all students in district and state standards.

❑ Step 3: Figure out a student's present level of educational performance with the standards in mind.

❑ Step 4: Develop annual goals based on a student's present level of educational performance as it relates to progress toward standards.

❑ Step 5: Examine previous IEP goals that do not seem to reflect progress toward standards.

❑ Step 6: Examine standards that are not addressed by any goals.

❑ Step 7: Document goals and standards on the IEP

❑ Step 8: Figure out how a student will participate in state and district assessments and document participation decisions on the IEP.

TABLE 5.2	**Test IEP Team Knowledge About State and District Standards**

Check the questions IEP team members can answer!

❑ What content or learning areas include your state standards?

❑ Are they the same at the district and state level?

❑ Are there grade-level benchmarks?

❑ How and where does instruction take place across the standards?

❑ Do students get "credit" for work toward standards that they do outside of the school building or school day? (See theater example in Chapter 3.)

❑ Which standards are assessed and at what grade levels?

❑ What other things are important to know before making decisions about the participation of individual students in standards and assessments?

(sometimes called functional, essential, foundational, or access skills) that are common to the instruction of students with significant disabilities and state standards and assessments. Some of this work has been piloted in some schools, but at this time, few states have made these connections statewide. Find out what has already been done in your state, and use it in developing standards-based IEPs with your students. If the connection has not yet been made, use the information in this book to get started. Send your work to people at the state level to help them get started.

Step 3: Figure out a student's present level of educational performance with the standards in mind.

Is the student working toward grade-level benchmarks? Some, but not all of them? If not, why not? What types of support have been used, and how did they work? These questions may be difficult to answer at first, because there may not be enough concrete information available to show a student's performance relative to standards. You may want to use a commercially available tool, like Lara's team did, to get started, especially with students whose goals were more maintenance than education oriented. Completed alternate assessments will provide valuable information for determining a student's present level of educational performance.

Step 4: Develop annual goals based on a student's present level of educational performance as it relates to progress toward standards.

This step gives much-needed direction to annual goals. For this step, ask the question, "Why does the student need special education services to progress toward educational standards?" As we saw in Chapter 2 (and the reason we keep going back to the information covered in Chapter 2), standards and goals are inseparable, and nearly all IEP goals can and should be linked to at least one standard. Go back to Chapter 2 as you think through this step. In that chapter, we worked on connecting goals to categories of standards and found that they were connected all over the place. Keep that information in mind here, as you use the standards to develop IEP goals.

Step 5: Examine previous IEP goals that do not seem to reflect progress toward standards.

Do goals that do not reflect progress toward standards show student learning? If not, can they be modified so that they can show progress toward a standard? For example, a student named Sara has an IEP goal that says, "Sara will be transported to the lunchroom by a peer." In an effort to match that goal to a standard, you might realize that it is not Sara's goal at all, it is the peer's, or it belongs to the teacher who scheduled the activity. As you look at it, though, you see that this activity could present an opportunity for Sara to work toward standards in connection with speaking and decision-making goals. What if Sara was learning to point to where she wanted to go (communication standard)? The peer could stop at the end of a hallway before turning and then go in the direction Sara pointed. Maybe Sara could have a choice about where she wanted to go, sometimes—for example, a choice between going to the library and going outside for recess (decision-making standard). She could point to where she wanted to go, and the peer could respond and push her in that direction.

We have been asked the question, "What about a student, like Lara, who is simply learning to chew and swallow food? That certainly couldn't be related to an academic standard." Hmmm, let's think about that one some more. What choices are involved in eating a meal? Making choices requires communication skills, whether to request a particular drink, choose between two vegetables, or spit out an undesired item. Is the student learning to use any assistive technology for eating? Many states have standards in tools and technology that a student might be working toward.

We are beginning to think that a goal that cannot be aligned with at least one standard is probably not a goal at all but a physical-maintenance activity. What do you think?

Step 6: Examine standards that are not addressed by any goals.

Standards are chosen by states and districts as critical competency areas for students to function successfully in their daily lives, both as children and later as adults. Is it OK

Box 5.6

— *Examples of States That Link IEP Goals to Standards*

State 1: In the instructions under "measurable annual goals," the final statement on this state's IEP form is, "Goals should reflect State Standards, when possible." This state's special education Web page is linked to the state standards page.

State 2: In this state, "Present Level of Educational Performance" includes the question, "How does this student perform within the general curriculum/content standards and on age-appropriate tasks and benchmarks?" "Annual goals" states that goals should reflect standards, key components, and access skills.

---

for some students to be exempt from making progress toward some of the standards? Which of the standards would it be fair to exempt them from? This is not to say that there should be an IEP goal for every standard. In states with 40 or more standards, that would mean at least 40 IEP goals!!! Going back to our example in Chapter 2 with all of the connections made for Tony's goals, it is clear that most goals can address several standards at once. Also, if the standards are compressed into more general learning areas (e.g., science or citizenship), the list probably will not total more than 10 learning areas, which could be addressed by as few as three or four carefully constructed goals.

Step 7: Document goals and standards on the IEP.

Some states have decided that all IEP goals must address standards (see Box 5.6), whereas others simply attach a list of standards to the IEP. Other state IEP forms show no connection at all between the IEP and standards or have not addressed it.

At the local level, if a state requires a particular IEP format and decisions have been made about how to address standards, then training needs to be provided about how to do this in ways that are most beneficial to students. If a state IEP form does not align goals to standards, then it is up to each district to figure out how to make this link.

IEP forms vary across the country, and within some states, even across districts. Standards may be addressed within the IEP, as an add-on, or not at all. It is important that IEP teams have a process that drives their planning and decision making and not be driven by items in the order that they appear on the form. In an attempt to meet but not exceed state and federal requirements (often as a backlash to excessive paperwork requirements), many states have streamlined their IEP forms so that they include no more or less than the specific requirements of the law. Often, rather than reducing paperwork, however, this has added to it extensively, because now, rather than having an IEP form that guides teams through a practical planning process, an additional form that sets up and explains the process is needed. IEP meetings that simply engage people in checking boxes on a streamlined compliance document may not result in plans that truly enable students to work toward standards or allow teams to make good decisions about participation in alternate assessments. Our best advice is to use the forms to fit the plan—don't try to develop a plan so that it will fit a rigid, compliance-oriented IEP form.

Lara's IEP Goals

Here are examples of some of Lara's IEP goals that show progress toward standards and were also assessed for her alternate assessment. Notice that the IEP goals are not the same as the standards. Standards give direction to IEP goals but are too general to be included as observable and measurable annual goals on Lara's IEP. Her actual goals are very specific to her needs and can be assessed as performance indicators on the alternate assessment. As you saw in the examples of connections between standards and goals in Chapter 2, each goal can show progress toward several standards, and each standard can be met through work on a variety of goals. Specific strategies for assessing these goals are described in Chapter 6.

Reading Standard: Students read a variety of materials, applying strategies appropriate to various situations.

Listening Standard: Students listen for a variety of purposes.

Tools and Technology Standard: Students use appropriate tools and technologies to model, measure, and apply the results in a problem-solving situation.

IEP Goal: Lara will look at and listen to a story that is being read to her and touch a switch to "read" a word from an icon when she sees and hears it in the text.

Tools and Technology Standard: Students use appropriate tools and technologies to model, measure, and apply the results in a problem-solving situation.

IEP Goals:
1. Lara will look at and listen to a story that is being read to her and touch a switch to "read" a word from an icon when she sees and hears it in the text.
2. Lara will touch a switch to turn on the light in her bedroom.
3. Lara will touch an automatic door switch to open a door.

Step 8: Figure out how a student will participate in state and district assessments and document participation decisions on the IEP.

The focus of Chapter 4 was on making assessment participation decisions, but we repeat that step here so you can see where it fits in the process of developing a standards-based IEP. One of the most important points we want to make in this book is that the assessment participation decision-making process needs to be viewed holistically—there is no way a team can just look at a checklist on a streamlined form meant to ensure minimum compliance to state and federal laws and just check off boxes without first carefully considering the questions asked in Figure 5.1.

STANDARDS-BASED VERSUS CLASSROOM-BASED ✖ —AN IMPORTANT DISTINCTION

Does participation in the general curriculum through standards mean that students have to sit in academic classrooms all day? One of the fears of addressing standards on the IEP is that a student's program might become very "academically" focused, taking away from opportunities to learn skills that would be useful to them as adults. The con-

Figure 5.1. Assessment Decision-Making Process

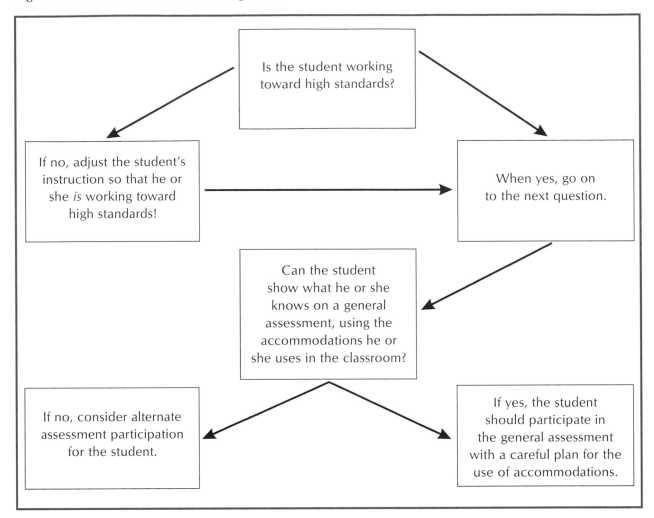

fusion often sounds something like this, "We have been working for years at building functional, age-appropriate community-based education services for students with severe disabilities. Are you telling us that we have to give it all up now and put them in general education classrooms to work on academic standards?"

This type of thinking is fundamentally flawed. It assumes either that learning academic skills is not useful or that the way students learn these skills in general education settings is not useful. Unfortunately, the way many skills have been taught in the past (using methods such as "drill & kill"), students with disabilities—and many other students as well—have not had opportunities to transfer skills from worksheets to real life. This is one of the problems school reform has set out to reform. High standards are meant to require students to *show* what they know and are able to do. Mathematics, for example, in a standards-based system, requires students to understand mathematical concepts and be able to use them in real-life situations. Those of us in special education have known for a long time that students with disabilities need to practice skills in real-life settings before they become useful. For example, learning to add numbers on a worksheet becomes useful only when a student can figure out whether he or she has enough money to buy CDs, groceries, clothes, or a bus pass.

Box 5.7

Amendments to the Individuals with Disabilities Education Act, P.L. 105-17 (1997)

"The term 'transition services' means a coordinated set of activities for a student with a disability that—(A) is designed within an outcome-oriented process, which promotes movement from school to post-school activities, including post-secondary education, vocational training, integrated employment (including supported employment), continuing and adult education, adult services, independent living, or community participation; (B) is based upon the individual student's needs, taking into account the student's preferences and interests; and (C) includes instruction, related services, community experiences, the development of employment and other post-school adult living objectives, and, when appropriate, acquisition of daily living skills and functional vocational evaluation."
(34 CFR §300.18)

We want to emphasize that we are not advocating for having students leave work sites to sit in classrooms and do worksheets; we are advocating for the work site to become the classroom—for students to have opportunities to work toward high educational standards across many settings to learn skills that will truly benefit them throughout their lives. Hopefully, those settings include students with a variety of abilities and disabilities, and both general and special educators, along with employers, other community experts, and parents, facilitate the learning that takes place in those settings.

TRANSITION-FOCUSED, STANDARDS-BASED IEPS

Since transition planning and services became law in 1992 (see Box 5.7), states have begun to implement rigorous educational standards, with high expectations for what students should know and be able to do by the time they leave high school. As evident in the previous chapters in this book, all students need skills for success in today's world. How better to achieve that success than to have a good plan for the future, a future based on high standards? Transition planning, working toward high standards and special education services are all about achieving success as an adult in today's world.

We have heard many people say, "Well, now that we have standards and alternate assessments, I guess we can't do transition planning anymore!" They wonder how they can cover yet another thing or write IEPs that are even longer. It is unfortunate that developing IEPs, helping students prepare for the transition from school to their adult lives (transition planning), and working toward standards were all mandated at different times. Because they were separate initiatives, they have often been placed in separate units within state departments of education and school districts, with training, instructions, and record-keeping documents that are completely separate or simply stapled together for compliance purposes. State agencies and large school districts might have different specialists in charge of each area, people who may not even know each other, much less work together. The NCEO recently reviewed IEP formats from every state and found that transition planning is completely separate from a student's education goals on most of the states' recommended or required IEP forms. Unfortunately,

Figure 5.2. Separate Initiatives

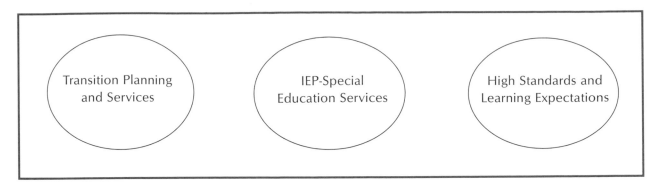

Figure 5.3. Integrated Opportunities for Learning

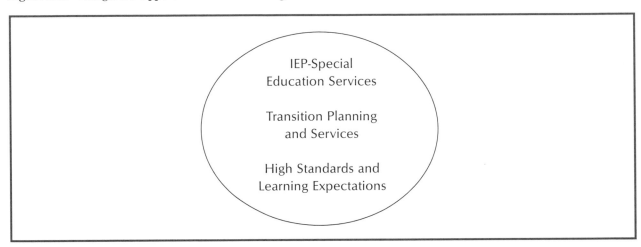

IEP formats are not set up to facilitate a practical transition planning process. They are designed to meet specific minimum requirements for documentation. No wonder so many teachers have been led to believe that these are all separate initiatives, like in Figure 5.2.

We want to expand what we know about building down-to-earth, commonsense, transition-focused educational plans with students with disabilities to planning that incorporates the best of a state's and district's educational standards. How can transition planning and high standards be related? We hope that we can help you think in terms of integrated opportunities for learning, as illustrated in Figure 5.3, and say, "How can they not be related?"

Transition Planning With Lara

Lara is 14 years old. Transition planning had not been mentioned at all, because until now, it had been expected that Lara would just go on living with her parents for the rest of her life (which no one expected to be very long) and that once she finished school, she would just stay home or go to the adult day care center. Employment or any type of community involvement was totally out of the question.

Once alternate assessments were required and it was determined that the school was now accountable for Lara's education, and once the teachers realized that she really could learn something useful, then they started thinking about how what she was learning could be enhanced to benefit her in the future. IEP team members began to wonder, for example, how Lara's new skill at using a switch could help her make choices and manipulate objects so she could experience some independence.

Lara's IEP team began looking for things she could do with a switch outside of the classroom. For example, could she learn to hit a switch on an automatic door to make it open? Could she turn her bedroom light on and off when she wanted to? Could she turn on her stereo or television set? Could they get a refrigerator door or a cupboard to open with a switch so Lara could choose a drink or snack? Being able to make choices with a switch and eye gaze could open up a whole world of future possibilities for Lara. And through alternate assessments, the team could show and be accountable for her progress.

IDEA was passed to ensure that "all children with disabilities have available to them a free appropriate public education that . . . prepares them for employment and independent living" (34 CFR 300.1(a)). In the past, the focus was on a free appropriate public education, but we have now added something equally important—preparation for a successful, satisfying adult life. IDEA challenges IEP teams to listen to a student's goals for the future and figure out what must be done to help a student meet those goals, both within the general curriculum by working toward high academic standards and through the support of the community. The challenge is to figure out how standards in the general curriculum can provide the best opportunities for students to work toward their transition goals. The order of planning is critical here. Rather than starting with the standards and figuring out how to fit a student with disabilities into them, transition planning begins with a student's personal goals and dreams for the future and then uses standards and supportive special education services to help the student meet those goals. For alternate assessment participants, this may mean the selection of performance indicators or skills within standards that are aligned with their goals for the future.

SETTING GOALS FOR ADULT LIFE ⊠

Preparation for high school graduation and life beyond school begins the first day a child enters a classroom. This preparation takes place through a process of gathering and using information to identify goals and strategies for learning that will increase the likelihood that young adults will succeed in life. It is based on negotiating plans with students that focus on their dreams, maximize their strengths, and minimize their limitations. Unless students have some sense of a vision for the future, the selection of standards to work toward, courses to take, extracurricular activities to participate in, and services such as special education may not work together to guide them toward a successful future.

The process of setting long-range goals with students can be accomplished through a number of strategies that take place on a regular basis throughout their school years, including

- Interviewing students individually
- Interviewing students with their parents or other family members over the telephone or in person

Box 5.8

▬ *State Standard for Interpersonal Communication*

"A student shall demonstrate the ability to communicate effectively in a small group by: solving a problem or settling a dispute; interacting and communicating appropriately with individuals of different gender, age, culture, and points of view; adjusting communication on the basis of verbal and nonverbal feedback; and expressing tone, mood, and vocabulary appropriate for a given situation."

- Completing a survey or checklist to work from during a planning meeting
- Discussing goals with students or parents (or both) within small-group instructional settings

In planning for the future, it is critical to listen to a student's hopes and dreams and then assess the student's skills in areas that will help move them toward their dreams. Including a student's family in the process of planning for the future is crucial. Sometimes, the goals and needs of different family members will be conflicting. There may also be times when family members disagree about what they believe is right for their child. Students, like Lara, who are unable to speak for themselves, need the support of everyone on their IEP team to help figure out a future plan with them.

Earlier in this book, we talked about the way IEPs used to include a laundry list of goals and objectives developed to help overcome a student's problems or deficits. There, we added a process that would help students work toward standards in ways that could then be assessed through alternate assessments. Now, we are going to take an additional step and focus that work toward standards within students' goals for their adult lives. In many states, this step has been taken, with standards developed that focus on skills students need as they make the transition to their adult lives. For example, one state has a standard for interpersonal communication that would be high on the list of any student looking at career or community participation goals (see Box 5.8).

✖ AN EFFECTIVE TRANSITION-PLANNING PROCESS

We have been involved in the design and implementation of a practical transition-planning process that takes advantage of everything schools and communities have to offer to help students meet their goals for adult life. This process has been used very successfully for the past 10 years with students across at least one state. A description of each of the steps follows:

Future goal-outcome: The first area to look at in a transition plan is a student's goals for life after high school. Because these are a student's goals, it makes sense to write them in a student's own words as much as possible. These goals can change and become more refined as a student has more experiences and gets closer to graduation. Students should have many opportunities to think about their future goals and to experience many options. In school, this means opportunities to work toward a variety of standards.

Present level of educational performance: Using a student's assessment information (including alternate assessment results), list the skills a student already has toward meeting future goals. These skills should cross several standards and relate to a student's future goals. Keeping this information positive will involve the student and family more and will give them the hope that they *do* have skills that will help them meet their future goals.

Transition services: List services and activities that will help students meet their future goals. Activities are things to do, in contrast to things a student needs to learn. Examples could include applying for Vocational Rehabilitation Services, calling for information about housing, taking a Community Education class, participating in general education classes that offer instruction toward standards, or participating in School-to-Work and other educational activities that will help students meet their goals.

Annual instructional goals and objectives: A student and his or her team thinks through present levels and needs and then prioritizes the things a student needs to learn into annual goals and objectives. Goals should take standards into account, as discussed earlier in this chapter.

Adaptations and accommodations: What will it take to help students meet their goals? Are readers needed? Is some type of technology needed? This is the "how" that supports the "what" addressed in previous steps.

The format in Form 5.1 may be useful as a guide to developing a transition-focused, standards-based IEP with a student.

There are many standards-based transition goals and activities that are important to address throughout middle and high school. Several examples are listed in Table 5.3. The examples are listed in the left column, with room in the right column to summarize your state or district standards. See how many connections you can make between the transition goals and activities and the standards. A transition plan for a student named Jeremy follows.

Jeremy's Standard-Based Transition Plan

Jeremy is 19 years old and assigned to the 11th grade. He attends a public school and has been in a program focused on functional skills his entire school career. Jeremy communicates with gestures and facial expressions. He doesn't have any intelligible speech. He is about 4 feet tall and gets around by walking, but his legs are badly bowed, so his gait is uneven and he doesn't move very quickly.

Having grown up in a foster home with other children experiencing disabilities even more limiting than his own, Jeremy has always been expected to do his share of work around the house and is very competent at housekeeping tasks, such as making his bed, loading the dishwasher, folding clothes, vacuuming, and dusting. His foster parents wisely knew that these were skills that would not only keep their household

Form 5.1. Transition-Focused, Standards-Based IEP Planning Guide

Future goal/outcome *(What I want to do after high school):*

Present level of educational performance *(What I can do now):*

Needs *(What I still need to do and learn):*

Activities *(What I plan to do to meet my goal, and who can help me):*

Annual goal *(What I plan to learn in the next year to meet my goal):*

Objectives *(Measurable steps toward meeting my annual goal):*

running smoothly but were also valuable employment skills that Jeremy could use in the future. Jeremy enjoys cleaning and seems very happy working on a job that he is familiar with and does well.

TABLE 5.3   Connecting Transition Goals and Activities to Standards

Transition Goals That Show Work Toward Standards (these are examples—use your students' goals)	Standards That Help Students Meet Transition Goals (these are examples—use your own state or district standards)
Learn strategies to improve study habits, time management, and general organization skills.	Resource Management
Become active participants in IEP meetings and begin to explore future goals in all transition areas.	Write and Speak
Become a self-advocate.	Read, Listen, View
Explore career interests and skills.	Fine Arts
Participate in service-learning opportunities.	Health and Physical Fitness
Request appropriate accommodations in school, home, work, and community environments.	Mathematics
Develop a profile of unique strengths and limitations.	Science
Get involved in community organizations, extracurricular activities, and school-to-work student organizations.	Citizenship
Participate in school-to-work activities.	Inquiry
	World Languages

Jeremy also enjoys everyday adult routines. For example, he starts his day with his feet up, having a cup of coffee, and looking at the newspaper. He doesn't have any reading skills but recognizes pictures of sports figures and ads for his favorite restaurants. He also likes to look good. He found a picture in a magazine of a hairstyle he liked and wanted, and after pointing to the picture and then to his head several times and smiling ear to ear, we finally figured out that he wanted his hair styled like the man in the picture. So with a fancy perm and style, Jeremy began to hold his head higher and actually seems a couple of inches taller!

Jeremy recognizes that money is a good thing and likes to have some in his wallet (which he always carries in his back pocket). He has learned what a quarter looks like and can put change in machines to buy coffee and a newspaper.

Jeremy is receiving vocational training as a housekeeper at a hotel. He uses picture cards to guide him through his tasks, with a job coach from school and other hotel employees to help creatively figure out how to get through daily challenges. For example, when Jeremy needs to get into a room, he knocks on the door and is supposed to say "housekeeping." He usually just makes a two-syllable noise and then giggles. One day, another housekeeper walking by during this routine, suddenly stopped and said to Jeremy, "Did you just say '*land shark*'?" (Referring to the guy on *Saturday Night Live* who knocks on the apartment door and says "land shark"—if you've ever seen it, you would smile as you read this!) Well, Jeremy just broke out in laughter when someone else actually caught on to his joke. From then on, the housekeepers all smile when they knock on doors, saying the required, "housekeeping," and thinking about their friend Jeremy's "land shark!"

Jeremy is a great cleaner and would like to work in a hotel (a fancy one!) as an adult. His team has decided that he can use a reading standard to help him work toward this goal so that he can follow pictorial directions and work more independently.

Reading Standard: Students read a variety of materials, applying strategies appropriate to various situations.
Goal: Follow directions in pictorial format.

One of the ways Jeremy can go about maintaining contact with his friends in the future is through E-mail. He can work on E-mail through the writing standard.

Writing Standard: Students write for a variety of purposes and audiences.
Goal: Create and send messages, such as greeting cards, pictures, and jokes, using electronic mail.

As an adult recreational activity, Jeremy's foster family would like him to attend community events with them and with his friends and relatives. This goal relates to the listening standard.

Listening Standard: Students listen for a variety of purposes.
Goal: Attend appropriately during large-group activities.

Jeremy's foster family wants him to be able to have some independent communication skills as he goes about his work, home, and community life as an adult. Jeremy has been working on using an augmentative communication device. He is working on this skill in the speaking standard.

Speaking Standard: Students speak for a variety of purposes and audiences.
Goal: Use an augmentative communication device to communicate.

✴ TRANSITION PLANS AND ALTERNATE ASSESSMENTS

What does transition planning have to do with alternate assessment? At this point, you may be wondering why we have spent so much time talking about transition planning when this book is about alternate assessment. We find that it is impossible to address alternate assessments without talking about standards, IEPs, and transition plans. The purpose of alternate assessments is to get a picture of how well students are progressing toward standards through all of their educational opportunities. Because alternate assessments primarily assess progress through performance-based measures (as you will read in Chapter 6), and because progress toward standards is addressed on IEPs, and because IEPs for older students become transition plans, it all fits together. The picture in Figure 5.4 may be helpful in showing the connection.

Figure 5.4. Connecting Learning to Assessment

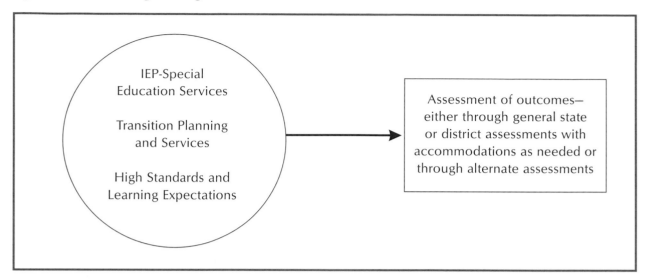

IN SUMMARY

Lara's IEP team admits that when they first heard that Lara's IEP needed to be standards-based, their reaction was, "Oh no, here comes another piece of bureaucratic paperwork we have to comply with." They were frustrated and angry because they were not familiar with standards, were comfortable with the way things were, and didn't see the purpose of this new mandate. After redesigning Lara's IEP so that it was focused on instruction toward standards and after seeing how much progress she could actually make toward those standards, the team has come full circle and is now planning with a purpose. For some, standards-based IEPs represent a big change in how they teach. This change is difficult and takes some time but, as in Lara's case, is well worth it for her education.

6

The Nuts and Bolts of Alternate Assessment Administration

TOUGH QUESTIONS

Most of my students don't complete pencil-and-paper assignments. How can I show what they're learning?

Who can collect data for an alternate assessment? What about parents, general education teachers, related-services people—is that appropriate?

Exactly what is a "body of evidence" for my students? Give me specific examples of what kinds of data are appropriate.

There are several strategies that can be used to gather data to show progress toward state or local content standards through alternate assessments. Each state has selected its own approach or, in some states, has given local districts the authority to do so. Most states compile data at multiple points over an extended period of time—usually most of a school year—using a variety of assessment strategies. Over half of the states organize the physical results of the data collected for a student's alternate assessment into some type of portfolio, whereas others summarize the results on a checklist or rating scale. A few states use a form to summarize progress on standards-based IEP goals for their alternate assessment. There are a variety of other recording methods used by a few states and within some districts. Regardless of the data collection method, there are typically three types of assessment strategies. These include observation, recollection (through interviews, surveys, or rating scales), or record review. These strategies are defined in detail by Salvia and Ysseldyke (2001) in the eighth edition of their book, *Assessment*. Of course, these strategies are useful with any student but are especially effective with students who are unable to show what they know and can do through traditional paper-and-pencil formats.

In this chapter, we use Salvia and Ysseldyke's (2001) framework to describe these strategies in relationship to the administration of alternate assessments. Following a discussion of assessment strategies, we discuss the compilation of assessment data into a portfolio or, as it is called in some states, a body of evidence. Even in states where a physical body of evidence or portfolio is not collected and scored by the state (for example, in states that use a checklist or IEP summary form), physical evidence of progress toward standards is needed to validate alternate assessment results. The chapter concludes with some "nuts and bolts," examples of ways to organize alternate assessment data as they are being collected across a school year. Take a look at Box 6.1 for ways to find out how your state collects alternate-assessment data.

▟ TYPICAL ASSESSMENT STRATEGIES

It is important to remember that *all* students can benefit from a variety of instruction and assessment strategies in daily classroom work. These assessments capture data that help us get a good picture of how every student is progressing toward standards. The use of a variety of assessment strategies, linked to instruction, can help us observe and monitor subtle or complex progress toward standards. For example, a variety of assessment strategies can help determine what learning is occurring for a student with the most challenging, multiple disabilities where progress is slow and subtle. Using a variety of assessment strategies also works for a student whose skills have gone far beyond basic competency in the standards, to complex levels of understanding and application that are not measured by selected responses or essay tests. Our focus in this chapter is on those students for whom progress may be subtle and defining desired results is a big part of the assessment challenge.

The assessment strategies described in this chapter are all qualitative; that is, they require some subjective judgment on the part of the assessor in collecting and recording data and in scoring results. At the end of this chapter there is a discussion about some issues that relate to the general category of the qualitative and subjective assessment approaches used in alternate assessments. Alternate assessments typically involve some variation of what is sometimes called performance-based assessment, authentic assessment, or "alternative" assessment, or with a collection of these tools, portfolio

Box 6.1

For More Information

You can find out more about how your state collects alternate assessment data in at least three ways:

1. Contact a special education official at your state department of education. Most states list their staff by program in a directory on their Web site.
2. Look for alternate assessment guidelines on your state education department's Web site.
3. Check out NCEO's Web site for publications on alternate assessment (*www.coled.umn.edu/nceo*).
4. If districts have the authority to decide how alternate assessment data will be collected, talk to a district person in charge of state or district assessments.

assessment. This chapter covers three typical assessment strategies: observation, recollection (through interviews, surveys, or rating scales), and record review.

OBSERVATION ✠

If you want to know whether someone can swim the length of a pool, you watch him or her swim the length of a pool. Observation, or watching someone do something, can provide accurate and detailed information. There are a couple of common ways to assess someone's performance through observation. The first is systematic, where the performance you want to observe is precisely defined ahead of time. You watch and record the frequency, intensity, or duration of the skill you are observing. Returning to our example of swimming the length of a pool, you might watch and record whether the person made it all the way from one end of the pool to the other. You might also watch and record the length of time it took, whether the person had to stop, and what types of swim strokes were used.

Another kind of observation is nonsystematic, where an observer just watches a person in a natural environment and takes notes on skills that seem relevant. For example, the observer might go to the pool and watch and record what a person does in the water. This type of observation is more subjective than systematic observation but may gather important information that might have been missed through a more formal observation. For example, maybe the observer found that it took the person about a half hour to get up enough nerve to get in the pool before beginning to swim or had difficulty breathing after swimming the length of the pool. To record observational data, you might observe a skill and complete a checklist like the one in the example in Form 6.1.

Once the information is recorded, judgments are made about the level of performance, based on some type of criteria or rubric. For example—not touching the bottom of the pool might score 4, touching once scores 3, and so on. Several states have physical fitness standards for which this type of observation might be relevant. Performance certainly could not be assessed through a paper-and-pencil test!

Form 6.1. Example of an Observation-Recording Form

Name of Student _____	Name of Observer _____			
Skill Observed: Swimming the length of a regulation-sized pool				
Skill	Date	Date	Date	Date
Length of time (seconds)				
Number of stops (feet touching bottom of pool)				
Type(s) of strokes (name)				
Other relevant observations				

Form 6.2. Example of Observation-Recording Form for Lara

Name of Student _____	Name of Observer _____			
Skill Observed: Physically activating a switch by touching it with hand				
Skill	Date	Date	Date	Date
Activate switch with physical prompt				
Activate switch with verbal prompt				
Activate switch independently				
Other relevant observations				

Let's look at an example for a student like Lara, a student for whom observations are more appropriate than paper-and-pencil tests. One of Lara's goals was to touch a switch that would then "read" a word in a book. This goal helped Lara work toward standards in both Reading and Tools and Technology. The specific skill for Tools and Technology was to physically activate a switch by touching it with her hand. A simple recording sheet, similar to the one shown in Form 6.1, might look like the example in Form 6.2.

Observational data also could be collected by videotaping, audiotaping, or by using photographs or slides. Assessors need to decide whether such taping would be continuous (and for how many minutes or days in a row) or snapshot style (e.g., every 3 hours for 10 minutes or every 3 days for 2 minutes). There are several advantages and disadvantages to the use of observation as an assessment strategy. These are described in Table 6.1

Observations can be conducted at school, home, in community settings, or on the job, depending on the skill being observed. Teachers, parents, job coaches, coworkers, peers who know the student well, or others could conduct observations. Table 6.2 shows steps for effective observations.

Let's look at an observation that clearly defines the skill to be observed and procedures for gathering information. We met the student described is this example in the previous chapter. Jeremy is a 19-year-old high school student. He is working toward a

TABLE 6.1 Advantages and Disadvantages of Observation Strategy	
Advantages of Observation Strategy	*Disadvantages of Observation Strategy*
Direct measure of actual skills	Observation takes more time than testing.
Avoids limitations of after-the-fact reporting	Students aware that they are being observed may change their behavior.
Widespread applications for many different settings	Observation depends on perception and judgment.
Suitable for use with students who are not disturbed by someone observing them	Halo effect (positive or negative bias based on a student's reputation) contributes to bias or error.
Better than formal testing for students with a limited response repertoire and unfamiliarity with testing situations	Reports may reflect the personality of the observer.

TABLE 6.2 Steps for Effective Observations

1. Pick the observation target.
   - Select one skill to observe.
   - Define the skill very clearly (e.g., "purchase soda from a vending machine using a dollar bill" *not* "on-task behavior" or "neatness").
2. Select observations settings.
   - Pick settings where skills naturally occur (e.g., watch a student making a purchase in a store with real money, rather than in a classroom setting with play money).
   - Use a variety of settings (e.g., vending machines in the cafeteria, at the ice arena, and at the recreation center).
3. Develop procedures for gathering information.
   - Determine when and where each observation will take place.
   - Specify who will observe.
   - Determine how data will be recorded.
   - Specify how observer reliability will be assessed.
4. Record observation right away (e.g., use paper and pencil, computer, videotape, audiotape).
   - Decide what to record (e.g., duration—how long skill lasts; latency—length of time between signal to perform and performance of skill; frequency—how often the skill occurs; and amplitude—intensity of skill.
   - Make sure the student is acting in usual ways (e.g., not "showing off" or "shying away") before recording the observation.
5. Verify observations.
   - Observe the skill at least three times.
   - Ask another person to observe performance of a particular skill (e.g., a teacher who does not usually work with a particular student, a parent, employer, or occupational therapist).

Reading Standard that says, "Students will demonstrate willingness to use reading to continue to learn, to communicate and to solve problems independently." Jeremy is working toward this standard in a vocational context and will show his progress by following directions in a pictorial format. You can see the list of specific skills that will be observed in the example.

Observation Example

Content Standard: Students will demonstrate willingness to use reading to continue to learn, to communicate, and to solve problems independently.
Setting: Vocational
Skill: Follow directions in pictorial format
Assessment Strategy: Observation

Observation is commonly used by members of Jeremy's IEP team to assess progress toward meeting IEP goals. In the Reading Standard, Jeremy is working on a goal in the vocational setting that requires following directions in pictorial form (photographs) to complete the routine of cleaning a hotel room. Jeremy is observed and rated on each step of the following eight-step sequence:

1. Clip set of cards and room key to belt loop
2. Gather supplies needed to clean room (card shows pictures of supplies)
3. Knock on room door and say "housekeeping"
4. Use key to enter room
5. Look at card and complete task shown
6. When the first task is complete, flip to next card
7. Continue routine of looking at next card and completing task
8. Take a break when all tasks are complete

Scoring: Weekly observation checklists are completed by Jeremy's job coach, work coordinator, or coworker. Scores are on a 4-point scale:

0 = *Unable to rate*
1 = *Does not or cannot do*
2 = *Does or can do with extensive assistance or supervision*
3 = *Does or can do with some assistance or supervision*
4 = *Does or can do independently*

Jeremy is observed completing each of the tasks and then scored. For scoring reliability, Jeremy's work coordinator, job coach, and a coworker take turns observing and scoring Jeremy performing the same routine. Scores are then compared and differences discussed.

RECOLLECTION

A second important strategy for collecting data on student performance involves the use of recollection through interviews, surveys, or rating scales. People who are familiar with a student can be asked to recall observations and interpretations of skill and events and can complete interviews, surveys, or rating scales based on their recollections. There are

TABLE 6.3	Advantages and Disadvantages of Recollection Strategy

Advantages	Disadvantages
Information gathered using this strategy is likely to reflect student performance in natural settings.	Skill is inferred from what informant chooses to reveal.
This strategy can be used to get a broad picture of a student's home environment and involves parents.	Questionnaires or rating scales may not allow opportunities for follow-up questions.
This strategy can provide information about situations and environments in which direct observation is difficult or impossible (i.e., past events).	Errors in reporting may occur because a child is not being directly observed.
For some assessment questions, informants may be the only source of information available.	Subjective information may be tainted by memory lapses and modifications of reality.
Measures used to gather data from informants are very flexible; they can access any setting and can be structured or open-ended.	The longer the time between the observation and recollection, the less accurate the memory of the skill.
This strategy may involve less time and be more cost efficient than direct observation.	This strategy is not well suited to measuring skill levels.
Checklists allow quick recording.	
Rating scales allow rater to assign a numerical value to responses instead of simply indicating whether a skill did or did not occur.	
Interviewer can clarify information or ask in-depth questions.	

several advantages and disadvantages of the recollection strategy. These are described in Table 6.3.

When interviews, surveys, or rating scales are used, data may be collected from the student (self-report or self-assessment); from peers; from teachers, therapists, or work experience coordinators; from employers; or from family members. A person who knows a student well might complete a checklist or scale with a student. Data could also be collected from peers. Other students might be asked to rate a student's performance on a particular skill. Peer ratings are especially helpful in rating development in areas such as interpersonal communication skills, social skills, or physical fitness. Most commonly, however, the information source would be a service provider (e.g., teacher, therapist, or work experience coordinator) or a family member.

Interviews may be conducted face to face, over the telephone, or in small groups. Interviews range in structure from casual conversations to highly structured processes in which the interviewer has a predetermined set of questions that are asked in a specific sequence.

Rating scales can be considered the most formal kind of interview. They enable data to be gathered in a structured, sequenced, and standardized way and facilitate data aggregation. One common kind of rating scale uses a Likert-scale format in which the rater responds to questions or statements by indicating extent of agreement with the

TABLE 6.4	Steps for Effective Recollections

1. Pick the recollection target:
   - Select skill(s) to collect information on.
   - Define the skill(s) very clearly (e.g., "purchase soda from a vending machine using a dollar bill" *not* "on-task skill" or "neatness").
2. Choose people who know a student well to provide recollections:
   - View an interview as a process of communication rather than a one-way street, with both parties receiving information from each other and providing responses to each other.
   - Remember that this information is subjective and should be interpreted with a "grain of salt."
3. Include these steps in an interview:
   - Introduction (get comfortable with the person being interviewed)
   - Focus (clarify the purpose of the interview and the information needed)
   - Information gathering (structure questions, clarify unclear answers, request further information)
   - Summary (paraphrase and reach consensus on information provided; close conversation).
4. Remember these points when constructing a survey or rating scale:
   - Include at least three points on the scale.
   - Make rating scales more specific than general skill inventories (to gather information about a specific skill).
   - Break the skill down into smaller parts. Ask a question about each part.
5. Verify recollections:
   - Observe skill at least 3 times.
   - Interview or survey another person to validate information.

---

statement (e.g., *strongly agree, agree, neutral, disagree, strongly disagree*). A second type of scale requires the rater to indicate the frequency with which specific skills occur. A third type involves rating the extent of assistance that must be provided and the settings in which the skill is exhibited (e.g., *does not do even with help, does with extensive help, does with minimal help, does independently*).

This approach can be made more sophisticated by indicating the settings (i.e., school, workplace, home, other) in which the student performs the skill. Another approach is to have a rater indicate the extent to which the student is consistent in demonstrating performance of the skill (e.g., *rarely or never shows skill* to *always shows skill*). The rater might also be asked to indicate the extent to which he or she is confident of the ratings.

Interviews may be conducted to make judgments about student performance of a skill based on information provided. Individually administered adaptive-skill scales are also useful sources of information that can be used to rate and make judgments about student development. A danger in the use of off-the-shelf adaptive-skill scales is identical to the danger for any and all published measures: Their content may not match a state's or district's content standards. Table 6.4 shows steps for effective recollections.

Let's look at a recollection that clearly defines the skill to be observed and procedures for gathering information, again with an example from Jeremy's alternate assessment. In the following example, the writing standard Jeremy is working on reads, "Students will employ a wide range of strategies as they write and use different written process elements appropriately to communicate with different audiences for a variety of purposes." Jeremy is working on this standard in a recreation-leisure setting and will show progress by creating and sending messages, such as greeting cards, using electronic mail. Interviews take place with Jeremy's classmate and with his brother.

Recollection Example

Content Standard: Students will employ a wide range of strategies as they write and use different written process elements appropriately to communicate with different audiences for a variety of purposes.

Setting: Recreation-leisure

Skill: Creates and sends messages, such as greeting cards, using electronic mail.

Assessment Strategy: Recollection, using interview format

Jeremy has an IEP goal that matches a skill for the Writing Strand in the Recreation-Leisure Setting. As a weekly activity, Jeremy and his friend Chris, a peer with reading and computer skills, create and send electronic greeting cards to friends who use the Internet. To assess Jeremy's ability to perform this activity, a special education teacher conducts a structured interview with Chris. Jeremy also does this activity at home with his brother, Sam. Sam meets with a special education teacher one day after school to be interviewed. Sam's responses are compared to Chris's.

Interview Questions

- Is Jeremy engaged in this activity? How do you know?

- How does Jeremy select a person to send a card to?

- Describe the process Jeremy uses to create and send greetings.

- On the following scale, how skilled is Jeremy at creating and sending greeting cards?

    ___ Beginner (1)

    ___ Partially Skilled (2)

    ___ Skilled (3)

RECORD REVIEW ✛

A third strategy for collecting data to show progress toward state or district standards is to pull together existing information through a review of records. There are at least five kinds of existing information, including (a) school cumulative records (including IEPs), (b) school databases, (c) student products, (d) anecdotal records, and (e) nonschool records. Use of these data sources requires development of standardized recording forms and procedures so that the information gathered is consistent and usable.

There are a number of limitations to relying on records to gather information about student achievement. First, it is usually necessary to go through a lot of information to find what is needed to answer assessment questions. The process can take a long time. Second, there is no control over data collected in the past. The person who recorded information decided what was relevant to record. Third, context formation is critical but

TABLE 6.5	Advantages and Disadvantages of Record Review

Advantages	Disadvantages
Information can be obtained from nonschool sources.	Person who records information decides what is relevant to record and may be biased.
Anecdotal records may supply a rich source of information.	Contextual information is typically not included in student records.
Records can give a historical picture of a student's progress.	Assessor has no control over information collected in the past.
IEP goals and objectives can be matched to skills.	It takes time to search through records for needed information.
	Quality of records varies.
	Information contained in records may not be current.
	Information needed may not be available in records.

usually impossible to evaluate. It is necessary to know the conditions under which a student demonstrated a skill or performed a task, but this information is not usually included in student records. Advantages and disadvantages of using record reviews are described in Table 6.5.

Cumulative records for students with disabilities or separate IEP files include copies of a student's IEPs and indications of the extent to which they are making progress toward the accomplishment of IEP goals, assessment results, multidisciplinary team evaluations, and information about student development. In some cases, a student database might be available for analysis (e.g., if student information on goal attainment is kept in a database for reporting purposes).

Besides cumulative records, student products might be a source of information about performance. Students produce many permanent products (e.g., drawings, writing samples, audio or video recordings). Some of these products are saved by teachers and, especially in the case of multiple products of a similar nature, over time can be used to judge progress.

Last, many teachers and therapists keep extensive anecdotal records about student performance, behavior, and physical status. With a little more work, information can be obtained from nonschool sources—parents, medical personnel, and others. This information can be used to make decisions about student performance. Steps for effective record reviews are shown in Table 6.6.

Another example of Jeremy's work toward standards follows and shows how record review is used as one of the methods for gathering information.

Record Review Example

Content Standard: Students will develop and apply the communication skills of listening, speaking, and viewing through a variety of informal and formal opportunities.
Setting: Community

TABLE 6.6	Steps for Effective Record Reviews

1. Pick the target to review:
   - Select skill(s) to review.
   - Define the skill very clearly (e.g., "purchase soda from a vending machine using a dollar bill," *not* "on-task skill" or "neatness").
   - Use anecdotal records and review actual products when available.
   - Use nonschool records where possible and appropriate (i.e., vocational rehabilitation plan, medical records).

2. Develop procedures for gathering information:
   - Decide which records will be used (look for information in records that is current, clear, objective, and measurable).
   - Determine who will do the review (be sure person reviewing records has permission to do so and confidentiality is maintained).
   - Specify how data will be recorded (clearly record sources of information).

3. Verify information collected:
   - Use multiple records when possible.
   - Have more than one person review the same records.
   - Validate information by checking with source when possible.

Skill: Attend appropriately during large-group activities.
Assessment Strategy: Record review

Jeremy's goal in this area is to attend group activities (e.g., school assemblies, church services, plays, and concerts) with his family and to listen attentively. In the past, Jeremy made loud, distracting noises during group activities, and the family had to take Jeremy outside. To assess this skill using record review, Jeremy's special education teacher looked at progress toward this goal on IEPs over the preceding 3 years. Progress was determined through a check sheet and reward system developed by Jeremy's teacher and parents. Progress over 3 years showed that Jeremy had gone from never being able to sit quietly through a group activity to making it all the way through about 3 out of 4 activities. Progress was recorded using the following scale:

0 = *No progress*
1 = *Minimal progress; needs lots of work*
2 = *Significant progress but still needs work*
3 = *Skill has been mastered*

COMBINING ASSESSMENT STRATEGIES ✺

These strategies can be combined in many ways. Here is one more example of Jeremy's progress, using both record review and recollection. This standard is a measurement standard that reads, "Student will apply measurement concepts to solve problems inside and outside the field of mathematics." Jeremy is working on this standard in an independent-living setting by using an alarm clock to get up in the morning. His progress has been recorded on his IEP in the past. Jeremy's special education teacher reviews past and current IEPs to determine Jeremy's performance level for this skill. Jeremy is also assessed on his performance of this skill using recollections.

Combining Assessment Strategies

Content Standard: Students will apply measurement concepts to solve problems inside and outside the field of mathematics.
Setting: Independent living
Skill: Use an alarm clock to get up at a designated time.

Assessment Strategy 1: Record review

Jeremy has been working on using an alarm clock to get up in the morning, to leave for school on time, and to take a break at work for the past year, and progress is recorded on the IEP. Jeremy's special education teacher reviews the IEP and determines Jeremy's performance level for this skill.

Assessment Strategy 2: Recollection

Jeremy's special education teacher asks Jeremy's mother how the alarm clock is working. Through this conversation, the teacher is able to rate Jeremy's current performance level. To increase reliability, Jeremy's father is also asked to rate progress. Because this skill takes place at home and would be difficult to simulate at school, Jeremy's teacher cannot observe progress directly and must rely on the family's recollection.

⁑ ALTERNATE ASSESSMENT PORTFOLIOS

An assessment portfolio is a purposeful and systematic collection of student performance assessments relative to standards (see definitions in Box 6.2). The collection is measured against predetermined scoring criteria and compiled into some type of file. Each portfolio entry consists of an assessment of a skill through the use of the assessment strategies previously described. Many states have selected a portfolio assessment as the alternate assessment mechanism for students with disabilities. Rather than calling this collection of work a "portfolio," some states and districts have chosen to call it a "body of evidence."

Here are some of the advantages states have listed in their decisions to compile alternate assessment data into a portfolio or body of evidence:

- Provides a broader picture of student achievement than tests
- Includes a variety of information that shows student progress toward standards
- Includes all students through an individualized process
- Demonstrates growth
- Increases the ability of schools to be more accountable for *all* students.

In selecting portfolio assessments, states have also considered these challenges:

Box 6.2
___

▬ *Definitions of Portfolio Assessment*

Perspectives on Policy and Practice (Northeast and Islands Regional Educational Laboratory, 1999):

"An assessment portfolio is the systematic collection of student work measured against predetermined scoring criteria. Portfolios are like a slide show that demonstrates student achievement, rather than the snapshot of student achievement that single-occasion tests provide." (p. 2)

A Teacher's Guide to Performance-Based Learning and Assessment (Educators in Connecticut, 1996):

"A portfolio is a purposeful collection of student performances that exhibits a student's effort, progress, and achievement over a period of time. . . . It is a way of tracking a student's progress on a variety of types of assessments throughout the year." (p. 118)

- Lower reliability and comparability than standardized tests
- Implementation more difficult and variable with portfolio assessments than with standardized tests (i.e., differences in the amount of support teachers provide to students, time allowed to spend on developing entries)
- Scoring portfolio assessments more difficult than scoring standardized tests (takes more time and may be difficult to obtain interrater reliability)

WHAT TO INCLUDE IN AN ✖
ALTERNATE ASSESSMENT PORTFOLIO

In our work with the development of alternate assessment portfolios, we have found three items that are useful for organizing and standardizing each student's portfolio: (a) an assessment portfolio checklist, (b) a student profile, and (c) an entry slip for each portfolio entry. Following is a description of each of these items, along with sample formats. Several states have already designed their own formats. As we have said before, check to see what your state requires before developing your own process!

Item 1: Assessment Portfolio Checklist

This checklist has three purposes: (a) to validate the decision to include a student in an alternate assessment rather than in the regular state assessment, (b) to be a reminder of what to include in the portfolio, and (c) to be an organizer or table of contents to assist the scoring team (see example in Form 6.3).

Item 2: Student Profile

The profile contains basic information about a student, including age and grade, educational background, current program, and unique characteristics (see the example in Form 6.4).

Form 6.3. Sample Assessment Portfolio Checklist

Name of person responsible for submitting portfolio _____

Participation validation: This student's IEP team has determined that this student is unable to participate in the general statewide assessment, even with accommodations, and will participate in the Alternate Assessment.

_____
Signature of parent or guardian

Use of portfolio entries for training: Permission is granted to use work contained in this portfolio for training on portfolio development and scoring for educators and contractors. Information identifying individual students will be removed prior to use.

_____
Signature of parent or guardian

(Check to make sure each item below is included before submitting assessment portfolio)
- ❑ Student profile

Entries that reflect achievement in English Language Arts *(this is the place to list the content areas and standards that the portfolio is expected to assess—also list the number of entries required in each area, for example, include a minimum of three entries per strand)*
- ❑ Writing
- ❑ Reading
- ❑ Speaking, listening, viewing

Entries that reflect achievement in Mathematics
- ❑ Number sense, properties, and operations
- ❑ Geometry and spatial sense
- ❑ Measurement
- ❑ Data analysis, statistics, and probability
- ❑ Patterns, algebra, and functions

Checklist of things to remember:
- This checklist is included in the front of this student's portfolio.
- Each entry is attached to a completed entry slip and all entries are dated.
- Standards assessed by each entry are checked on each entry slip.
- The required number of entries are included for each strand.
- A variety of assessment strategies are used and students are assessed across a variety of settings.

Form 6.4. Sample Alternate Assessment Portfolio Student Profile
(Include in front of Assedssment Portfolio)

Student Name _____ School _____

Portfolio Beginning and End Dates _____

Age _____   Grade *(circle one)* 4 6 8 11

Other Classifications *(circle)*   Limited English Proficient   High Mobility

Accommodations or assistive technology regularly used (describe below):

Communication

Mobility

Other

Unique characteristics of student (strengths, needs)

Item 3: Entry Slips

An entry slip precedes each portfolio entry and includes information about what the student was asked to do, what standards the work assesses, assessment strategies, entry format, level of assistance, and additional comments. To standardize the entries and make sure that they address specific standards, it may be helpful to list the standards and skills on the back of each entry slip (see the example in Form 6.5).

Suggestions For the Administration of Alternate Assessment Portfolios

Alternate assessment portfolios are designed as a tool to collect and organize data to assess student progress toward standards. If a state assesses student achievement through criterion-referenced tests in the areas of English Language Arts and Mathematics, the alternate assessment portfolio would contain entries showing a student's skills across standards in English Language Arts and Mathematics. To collect a body of evidence for an alternate-assessment portfolio, educators who work with each alternate assessment participant generally collect information throughout the school year until the criterion-referenced assessments are administered in the spring.

Form 6.5. Sample Alternate Assessment Portfolio Entry Slip

Student Name _____ Date _____

Entry slip completed by _____

Exactly what was the student asked to do?

Check *all* standards and skills addressed by this entry (*on back*). If the skill addressed by this entry is not listed on the back of this form, please write it here: *Grade* _____   *Standard* _____

Skill _____

Assessment strategy(s) used (*check below*):
❑ Observation   ❑ Recollection   ❑ Record review

Entry format (*check below*):
❑ Student work–paper   ❑ Record-keeping form   ❑ Related IEP goal page
❑ Audiotape   ❑ Videotape   ❑ Computer diskette
❑ Photographs   ❑ Other (*describe*) _____

Level of assistance (*check below*):
❑ Independently initiated   ❑ Teacher or other initiated   ❑ Few verbal prompts
❑ Several verbal prompts   ❑ Responds to gestures   ❑ Some physical assistance
❑ Extensive physical assistance ❑ Tolerates or cooperates passively ❑ Other _____

Comments (*anything else that will help a rater understand this entry*)

There are several practical suggestions for administering alternate assessment portfolios. We have listed these and have added examples of forms and worksheets that could be adapted to individual situations and used as organizing tools.

Suggestion 1: Decide who is primarily responsible for compiling entries with a student —don't assume someone else is doing it, and don't try to do it alone! Encourage students to play a role in collecting and displaying their own work. As you work with other partners in thinking this through, help all partners focus on the *student,* perhaps by using communication tools like the example in Form 6.6.

Form 6.6. Sample Communication Tool

To My Teachers (tailor to each partner)

Hi, I'm going to be learning in your classroom (tailor to each partner)
this year. Here's some *key* information that will help me be successful.

_____

(student "signature" of some type here)

Name:

Here's what I can do the best:

Academics:

Behavior:

Motor skills:

Here's what I am working on:

Skills that link to standards, helpful accommodations

And one question for you that is key to my learning:

What can I do in your classroom to help me gather data for my alternate assessment portfolio to show others what I'm learning?

Form 6.7. Planning Worksheet for Alternate Assessment Portfolios

Partners in general education, related services, community settings, and at home can conduct assessments to use as entries in an alternate assessment portfolio.

Standard:

Specific skill that shows progress toward the standard:

Setting:

Instructional strategies, accommodations, modifications:

Assessment strategies, entry formats—who gathers it, what does the evidence look like, when will the entries be collected (see calendar):

Relationship to IEP goals and objectives:

Suggestion 2: Get related-services specialists and general education personnel involved in collecting portfolio entries—do not do all of the work in the special education class-room. Anyone involved in a student's education—speech clinicians, occupational thera-pists, physical therapists, work experience coordinators—can collect portfolio entries. (Review the roles of partners back in Chapter 3.) Form 6.7 shows another way to organize the work of each partner.

Suggestion 3: Use multiple assessment strategies that show progress toward specific standards—this is an assessment portfolio, not just a collection of classroom work. Use a combination of the assessment strategies described earlier in this chapter, and work across multiple settings and partners to show the richness of each student's learning.

A calendar like the sample in Table 6.7 can help you plan.

TABLE 6.7	Conducting Assessments Across Standards: Calendar of Who, What, Where, and When							

Standard Month	Writing	Reading	Speaking, Listening, Viewing	Number Sense	Geometry, Spatial Sense	Measurement	Statistics, Probability	Patterns, Algebra, Functions
September								
October	OT-PT		S	C		RR		
November		RR			H		C	GE
December			GE	C		RR		
January	OT-PT					GE, H	H	
February		GE			RR			GE
March	OT-PT		S, GE			GE	C	
April		RR, H		C	H			GE
May								

Settings codes:
  RR = Resource Room
OT-PT = Therapy settings
   S = Speech
  GE = General Education—with annotations as necessary as to which classroom
   C = Community—with annotations as necessary as to work, recreation-leisure, and so on
   H = Home

Many portfolio assessment entries reflect more than one standard. For example, assessments for the Measurement and Patterns, Algebra, and Functions standards are conducted in both special education resource and general education classroom settings. Similarly, Speaking, Listening, and Viewing can be assessed both by a speech clinician and by a general educator.

Suggestion 4: Use a variety of different entries—don't use worksheets or multiple-choice tests! (Students who can take multiple-choice tests should be in the general assessment, not the alternate.)

Suggestion 5: Use a student's own work—don't include work that has been edited, improved, or copied by someone else! (This is an assessment of the student's work—"fixing it up" will invalidate the assessment.)

Suggestion 6: Include entries that reflect a student's progress toward standards—don't write notes on work that reflect timeliness, neatness, completeness, or other skills unrelated to the standard being assessed.

Suggestion 7: Collect portfolio assessment entries on a regular basis—don't wait until the last minute! (You will be overwhelmed, and the portfolio won't reflect a student's progress throughout the year.) Table 6.8 shows an example of one way to organize an alternate assessment portfolio across a year.

Suggestion 8: Date and label everything in the portfolio right on the work itself (e.g., on audiotapes and videotapes, computer files, and photographs) and match the work to a specific entry slip—don't make raters hunt and guess! Confusing work may reduce the reliability of a student's score.

Suggestion 9: Clearly identify all information included on a rating sheet or checklist—again, don't make raters hunt and guess! A legend or key to show what symbols represent, a description of exactly what is being charted, and a label on each axis of a graph are essential for scoring. Before including your forms in the portfolio, check out their clarity with someone who has never seen them.

Benefits and Challenges to the Use of Portfolios for Alternate Assessments

Just as there is no consensus about how to deliver standards-based instruction, there is no consensus about how qualitative assessment, used to collect a body or portfolio of evidence, fits into the larger picture of assessment and accountability or how to implement the portfolio assessment process to ensure high-quality results. Salvia and Ysseldyke (2000) caution that subjective and qualitative measures have a number of technical issues that must be addressed. These include the following:

- How the content will be selected for inclusion in the portfolio
- What quality of work to use (e.g., best work vs. typical work)
- Whether students should participate in selecting items
- How much information is needed to get a true score

In addition, scoring of portfolios is, according to Salvia and Ysseldyke (2000), "neither simple nor straightforward," (p. 248) nor are score aggregation or score reliability issues resolved. Yet they suggest that attention to "greater objectivity, less complexity, more scorer training, and greater comparability of portfolio contents are the keys to better practice" (p. 257).

Stiggins (2000) also addresses this challenge of ensuring high-quality assessment data from portfolio assessment. He suggests that professional and subjective judgment plays a key role in determining the quality of performance assessment and that setting clear standards of achievement against which you measure is as key a decision as you will make. He cautions the practitioner,

It is your vision that you will translate into performance criteria, performance tasks, and records of student achievement. For this reason, it is not acceptable for you to hold a vision that is wholly a matter of your personal opinion about what it means to be academically successful. Rather, your vision must have the strongest possible basis in the collective academic wisdom both of experts in the discipline

TABLE 6.8	Time Line and Suggestions for Alternate Assessment Portfolio		
Time Line	*IEP Process and Linkages*	*Gathering Data*	*Portfolio*
September	Review each student's IEP and look for opportunities to link ongoing instruction and assessment to portfolio data requirements—that is, identify what the student is already doing in a variety of settings that can be used to demonstrate progress toward standards; then, identify gaps; and develop a plan to fill gaps.	Provide key information to classroom teachers and related services providers; ask for their ideas on data collection. Based on ideas received from key information, develop a plan and propose a time line for gathering data from all settings—across strands, three to four pieces per month.	Gather folders, entry sheets, other materials. Consider hosting a parent information meeting for all parents of portfolio students in your school. Consider presenting basic information about portfolio requirements to a staff meeting.
October	Work with partners to refine instructional strategies for selected skills in each setting—remember that more than one standard can be addressed in one activity or in more than one setting.	Gather monthly collection of student work from all cooperating staff and family.	Select appropriate work for inclusion, provide feedback to cooperating staff to improve work samples, share ideas to improve learning opportunities. Pose questions you have to district and state staff.
November	Instruction continues in all settings, consistent with IEP decisions.	Refine data collection plan based on first month's data.	Participate in any available training
December	Monitor progress.	Gather monthly collection of data.	Select appropriate work for inclusion, provide feedback to cooperating staff.
January	Review instructional plans, monitor progress, adjust instruction if needed.	Gather monthly collection of data.	Select appropriate work for inclusion, provide feedback to cooperating staff.
February	Monitor progress.	Gather monthly collection of data.	Participate in any available training; select appropriate work.
March	Monitor progress.	Gather monthly collection of data.	Select appropriate work for inclusion, provide feedback to cooperating staff.
April	Cross-check IEP requirements with finished portfolio.	Meet with partners to assemble all pieces into final portfolio.	Participate in any available training; conduct final selection of appropriate work.
May	Review portfolio with partners; prepare for next year.	Distribute student thank-you notes to all partners.	Review results; plan for next year.

within which you assess and of colleagues and associates in your school, district, and community." (p. 188)

Having time as a teacher to study the current thinking of the research community, as well as having time to work with colleagues in developing better understanding, is critically important and not always feasible.

Yet training of staff involved in performance assessment is the key to improved results for teachers and students. Gersten, Chard, and Baker (2000) reviewed the literature on sustainability of classroom innovation in special education and developed a set of sustainability factors and issues. They include the following six items:

1. A deliberate plan for training, coaching, modeling

2. Realistic time lines and implementation processes

3. Opportunities for teachers to think through how the new practice fits their students and their local context

4. Availability of peer networks and support and collegial learning opportunities

5. Administrative support

6. Explicit links between the innovation and student performance

Leaders in any change effort, including alternate assessment, need to think through these issues if they hope to achieve sustainable change.

These cautionary tales are not meant to discourage use of performance assessment or portfolio assessment, because there is a large body of high-quality material and training to build the skills that general and special education teachers need. Wiggins and McTigue (1998); Rogers and Graham (2000); and Newmann, Secada, and Wehlage (1995) are just a few examples. But states and districts can and must support the efforts of teachers and their partners in developing high-quality skills at authentic, performance-based, or portfolio assessment if the use of alternate assessment is going to meaningfully improve the outcomes for student with the most significant disabilities.

7

Scoring, Reporting, and Using Alternate Assessment Data

TOUGH QUESTIONS

Isn't special education only responsible for improvement of schooling for students with disabilities? Why would we want to be involved in our school's improvement processes for general education?

How can scores from alternate assessments fairly reflect both student progress against a standard and student progress against individualized student needs and abilities? Wouldn't all students participating in alternate assessment automatically score at the lowest level in state reporting systems?

What do the results from alternate assessment mean?

✖ USING DATA FROM ALTERNATE ASSESSMENTS

Once we have gathered a body of evidence on each student's progress toward standards, what do we do with it? In most states and districts, the next steps are as follows:

- Scoring the alternate assessment
- Integrating the scores from the alternate assessment into school and district reports that include all students
- Reporting results to the public
- Using the data to improve instruction

Here again, we find that students with disabilities, especially those with the most significant disabilities, are often left out of the cycle. Students with disabilities may be included in assessments, but the assessments are not always scored, included in reporting, or used in school improvement processes. Why should we care? The most important reason to care is that most states are requiring a data-based decision-making process for school improvement for all schools. If some students aren't represented in the data, they will also not be represented in efforts to improve instruction and outcomes. There is a saying "We treasure what we measure," or alternatively "We measure what we treasure." If we "throw away" data for some of our students, we also risk throwing away opportunities for those students. As a bottom line, including students with disabilities in assessment and accountability systems ensures that they will be included in budgetary systems as well.

The most important reasons, however, relate back to the opening statements in our book:

- All children can learn.
- All children thrive in an atmosphere of high expectations about what they will learn.
- If all children are expected to learn, and they have had opportunities to reach high expectations, all children can be successful.

If we believe these statements, then the results for all students need to be scored, counted in the reporting of results, and used to improve schooling. In this chapter, we develop a way to ensure that data from alternate assessments are used to improve schools as well as to improve instruction for individual students.

The reasons we need to do this come to life when we talk about the lives of real people. Consider the consequences involved in each of the following scenarios.

A Student View

▬▬▬▬▬▬▬ Until Lara was 14 years old and included in her state's assessment system, no one was held accountable for Lara's education. Her teachers, other educators in her school, related-services personnel, and even her family assumed that she was incapable of learning. Based on the results of the assessment, the schools were able to redesign their programs and services for students with significant disabilities around high expectations. How much more progress might Lara have made over all of those years if she had been included in the assessment and accountability system from an early age?

A Teacher View

Paul Jones teaches 4th grade. Of the 23 students in his class, 2 receive special education services for fairly significant cognitive disabilities. Paul was told by the school administration that he would receive a bonus if all of his students did well on the state test. He was also told not to worry about the two special education students. They would not be tested, so he could get the bonus no matter how they did.

What should Paul do? What is his incentive to make sure every student in his class does well? He might be the kind of teacher who motivates all of the students in his class to do their best, or he might be really concerned about receiving that bonus so he could put a new roof on his house over the summer. How much attention does he need to pay to the progress of the two students who don't count anyway?

What if the two students with disabilities were included in the assessment through an alternate assessment and Paul was told that their performance would count as much as the other students in his class? Would Paul ask that those students be transferred to someone else's class? Might he work harder than ever to make sure they were achieving to high standards, just as he did for everyone else in his class? Maybe he would see a need to collaborate more closely with the special education staff to make sure everything possible was being done to help the students make progress toward high standards.

A School View

Policymakers at North Senior High School are considering adding more advanced-placement (AP) classes for students with high grades and test scores. During planning for the district standardized tests, school staff were told that only students who were expected to do well needed to participate in the assessments, to help plan the number of staff and classrooms need for the new AP courses. Once the tests were given and the AP staff and classrooms allocated, it was found that there were not enough staff and classrooms left for the lower-performing students. Because the district's goal was to emphasize opportunities for their high-performing students, the remaining students were placed in overcrowded classrooms with the least qualified staff. For example, a "general Math" class had 45 students in a room meant for 30, with a teacher who was only certified in physical education.

District officials were baffled when confronted by a group of concerned parents who asked how they could justify treating students differently. The parents wanted to know what data they had to show that all students were being held to high standards and were making progress toward those standards. The school board members wondered out loud, "How did we end up in this situation? Are the lower-performing students making progress? Does anyone know? Are we accountable for those students, too?"

A Parent View

Cindy was always in special education. Even in high school, all of her textbooks were the same as those used in the 3rd grade, because that was determined to be her reading level. Her special education teachers were not included in the development or implementation of state standards, and when test time came around, Cindy was given the 4th-grade test, but her scores were pulled and destroyed. In Cindy's state, students had to pass a series of criterion-referenced tests based on the state standards to graduate with a diploma. Because Cindy wasn't working toward any standards and did not take the test for her grade level, it was assumed that she would not get a diploma, just a certificate of completion.

Her parents always wondered if the situation could have been different. They had found at home that when they read to Cindy, she seemed to absorb a lot more information than anyone at school ever thought she could. What if Cindy had been working toward high standards with accommodations and support from special education all along? Could she have eventually taken the graduation test successfully? Could she have been included through the alternate assessment so that the school would have been accountable for her progress toward standards? By leaving her out, no one would ever know.

How do we define "success" for students with the most significant disabilities? That brings us to a discussion about how the alternate assessment is scored and how it fits into the assessment data reports (see Box 7.1). Generally we need to think about rubrics, performance levels, and reporting processes to understand how states are similar and different in their approaches.

✕ SCORING ALTERNATE ASSESSMENTS

For most performance-based assessments, we use scoring rubrics to define specific criteria for each sample of student work. We all have experience using scoring rubrics, without even using the term. When we look at a travel guide to determine where to eat or where to spend a night, we often use a rubric—perhaps one to four "stars" to help us make our choice. The rubric for a motel may include measures of how clean it is, how many services it offers, or even how comfortable the beds are! These are criteria often used to evaluate the level of quality of a motel for someone making a choice about where to stay. These are also criteria against which the motel managers measure their own success and from which motel managers develop plans to improve. As individuals, we place different emphasis or value on the criteria for motel quality—one person may see cleanliness as the highest value; another will choose a motel based on services, such as whether it has an indoor pool.

The use of rubrics in measuring success for students participating in alternate assessments is similar in that states and districts set some common criteria that are used to measure quality and level of success of the student portfolio or body of evidence. These criteria may include dimensions such as the following:

- How well a student can perform target behaviors or skills
- What level of independence a student demonstrates
- How well the skills are generalized to different environments, with different people, or in different activities
- How appropriate the skills and activities are for a student

By looking at a body of evidence that demonstrates student performance and comparing what is shown with criteria like these, we can "score" the overall performance of students against the criteria. But across states, districts, and schools, and even within schools, we find that different values are placed on how success is measured for students with significant disabilities.

Box 7.1

━ *Technical Issues in Scoring and Reporting Alternate Assessments*

To understand how we score alternate assessments, we have to think briefly about some basic measurement principles. In Chapter 6, we referred to technical issues of scoring of portfolios because of the subjective and qualitative nature of the data. There are a number of researchers who have posed questions about how to ensure reliability and validity in the use of portfolio assessment (Custer, Schell, McAlister, Scott, & Hoepfl, 2000; Shepard, 2000; Taylor & Nolen, 1996). These discussions suggest that the concepts or reliability and validity do not have precisely the same meanings for portfolio assessment as they do for pencil-and-paper large-scale assessments. These writers explore the interaction of assessment and instruction and call for thoughtful rethinking of quantitative models of reliability and validity as we work toward more systematic use of qualitative methods for large-scale assessment. Koretz, Stecher, Klein, and McCaffrey (1994) suggest,

> Despite common rhetoric about "good assessment being good instruction," we believe that the tension between the instructional and measurement goals is fundamental, and will generally arise in performance assessment systems that either embed assessment in instruction, rely on unstandardized tasks, or both. This appears not to be a problem that can be fully resolved by refinements of design; rather, policymakers and program designers must decide what compromise between these goals they are willing to accept.

As we work with alternate assessment, it will be helpful to remember that this compromise between goals affects how alternate assessments are scored across the states and how "success" is defined. In the meantime, there may not be simple solutions to the challenges of resolving the technical issues of reliability and validity in the scoring and reporting of alternate assessments for students with significant disabilities. It will be extremely important to thoughtfully and continuously improve the processes as we learn more.

VALUES REFLECTED BY STATE SCORING RUBRICS ✖

States incorporate their values into rubric content and scoring. For example,

- Many states focus on specific skill development in literacy and numeracy and limit scoring to evidence that shows *level of skill* demonstrated in the performance, sometimes using banks of common tasks from which to choose or a checklist to complete.

- Some states focus on *multiple dimensions of student skills*, such as appropriateness of skills, numbers of settings where the student demonstrates skills, the level of independence or support the student needs to do the skill, and the numbers and quality of student interactions with peers and adults.

- Other states emphasize that IEP teams must thoughtfully and creatively link student goals to content standards, but their scoring mechanism is limited to the dimension of *level of independence regardless of skills* being targeted or linkage to standards.

- Still other states count *numbers of skills, job activities, prompts, and settings* evident in the body of evidence and use parent observations of the accuracy of the work samples as controls for reliability and validity.

Regardless of how the scoring rubric is developed, in most states, once the alternate assessments are completed, a scoring process takes place to rate each student's work. These processes vary greatly, for example:

- In states with a teacher-generated checklist as the primary assessment tool, teachers generally score their own students and submit the scores to the state with no state oversight.
- Another option is for teachers to score their own students' work. Following this, the state samples a percentage of the work samples to rescore and report.
- Teachers are trained to score all the student work, but no one scores his or her own students or own district work, followed by expert rescoring of a sample of work.
- In some states, regional panels review all portfolios with at least two independent scores, and expert scorers rescore those portfolios whenever the original two scores are in disagreement.

Each of these approaches has strengths and weaknesses, and we anticipate that as alternate assessments are fully implemented, we will see many changes in scoring procedures. After setting criteria, developing rubrics, and scoring the evidence, another step is taken to refine the levels of performance against the content and performance standards.

⊞ SETTING PERFORMANCE LEVELS

We think of assessment scores as a finite measure of success—perhaps a 75% percentile, or 80% correct, or even Pass or Fail. In most states, measurement of student progress against standards is translated into a performance level of proficiency. For example, a typical state may have three to five performance levels, such as the following: 4 = *Advanced level*, 3 = *Proficient level*, 2 = *Below proficient*, 1 = *Not proficient*, 0 = *Not measureable, not scored*.

Usually, in a large-scale assessment, actual scores on the assessment are translated into these levels, often by groups of stakeholders and technical committees who define the score ranges that reflect levels of achievement. For performance assessments, these stakeholder and technical committees identify examples of student work that can serve as anchors and exemplars that demonstrate what a "1" looks like, what a "2" looks like, and so on. Over time, the definitions of performance levels firm up and are more easily communicated to all stakeholders.

Similarly, states and districts work to develop a common understanding of levels of performance for students participating in alternate assessments. In Chapter 2, we explored the ideas that content and performance standards may be the same for all students; but performance indicators that demonstrate progress toward the standards will vary for students who have many challenges for learning. We called these teacher-developed performance indicators the "high expectation" bridge between the state content and performance standards and the needs and abilities of students with the most significant disabilities. In most states and districts, stakeholders and technical committees have to decide whether the performance levels for the alternate assessment will reflect the absolute standard held for the general assessment or whether they will reflect a relative standard based on the high expectation bridge between state content and performance standards and the needs and abilities of the individual student.

In some states, the performance levels of the alternate assessment reflect exactly the same expectations as the general large-scale assessment, and almost all alternate assessment participants score at the lowest level against the standards. These states emphasize the measurement *against absolute standards* over the relative emphasis on individualized needs and abilities. In these states, most students participating in the alternate assessment are performing at the "0" or "1" level.

Other states have a separate definition of performance levels for the alternate assessment that emphasizes student-by-student growth of skill toward the *relative standard based on the high-expectation bridge,* which does not reflect comparison to absolute standards. Students in the alternate assessment may be assigned a level of "advanced" or "4" if the body of evidence shows outstanding progress in skill against the student's own needs and abilities. Many of these states use the IEP as the baseline for each student's growth.

There are many variations to how levels are determined across the states, and the beliefs and philosophy of the state stakeholders typically drive these decisions. The potential for misuse of the data exists if the public, parents, educators, and the media do not understand how and why these decisions were made. And if the scores of all students participating in the alternate assessment are "0" or "1," how can the scores and resulting reports be used for school improvement planning? What do they mean? And alternatively, will we lower expectations for these students if we introduce a relative standard in defining performance levels? We will return to this point later in the chapter when we discuss audiences for the information.

The state of Kentucky has been a pioneer in the use of alternate assessment and can be considered the leader in research and practice regarding scoring and reporting of alternate assessment results. Its online materials (*www.ihdi.uky.edu/projects/KAP*) and its Web site linkages to other organizations are invaluable. For example, a study was done in the state of Kentucky about the impact of alternate assessments (Kleinert, Kennedy, & Kearns, 1999). The results of this national survey clearly indicated that (a) experts in education programs for students with severe disabilities believed strongly that alternate educational assessments should be based on the same learner outcomes (or a subset of those learner outcomes) identified for all students and that (b) although students with significant disabilities may evidence those same outcomes in adapted ways, we should be careful that our functional interpretations of those adapted ways do not result in lowered expectations or a narrowing of curricular options for these students.

Several states use the alternate assessment scoring process as an important staff development activity. Box 7.2 offers a rationale for this staff development process.

REPORTING ASSESSMENT RESULTS ✖

To understand how reporting assessment results affects students, we need to revisit the key components of standards-based reform. Under federal law and in practice in all states, all students are expected to work toward the same high expectations or standards.

Box 7.2

▬ *Scoring Alternate Assessments as a Staff Development Strategy*

When general and special education teachers are brought together with portfolios of student work from across the state, it gives them a chance to see what other teachers are doing and to share instructional strategies. Teachers say they learn the most about administering alternate assessments through involvement in a scoring process. By carefully reviewing student work assembled by other teachers, it becomes clear what kinds of assessment strategies are effective in demonstrating the richness of what a student knows and is able to do. Given the discussion in Chapter 6 about how important it is for each teacher to develop skills in defining student learning tasks and records of achievement for high-quality performance assessment, this kind of staff development is essential to a high-quality alternate assessment. Stiggins (2000) suggests to teachers that for high-quality performance assessment, "your vision must have the strongest possible basis in the collective academic wisdom both of experts in the discipline within which you assess and of colleagues and associates in your school, district, and community" (p. 188). Scoring opportunities give teachers the kind of collective learning experience that is needed and meets the need for thoughtful scoring at the same time!

Box 7.3

▬ *Letter and Attachment (Summary Guidance on the Inclusion Requirement for Title I Final Assessments) from Assistant Secretary for Elementary and Secondary Education Mike Cohen (April 7, 2000)*

"Whatever assessment approach is taken [referring to standard assessment, assessment with accommodations, or alternate assessment], the scores of students with disabilities must be included in the assessment system for purposes of public reporting and school and district accountability." (Attachment on Summary Guidance, p. 2)

States and districts must measure how well students are doing by using assessments that are aligned to standards. Based on assessment results, school improvement teams work to improve curriculum and instruction so that all students can succeed. States, districts, and schools are accountable for the results of all children, and looking at the assessment results tells us whether schools are moving in the direction of success for all children. Assessment is a process of collecting data for the purpose of making decisions about improving schools or student progress. Assessment includes options such as large-scale tests and assessment portfolios.

A primary method of assuring everyone inside and outside educational systems that students are making progress toward the same high expectations or standards is by reporting assessment results for all students. Title I (see Box 7.3) and IDEA (see Box 7.4) both specifically require reporting of results for all students, including students with disabilities.

Box 7.4

— *Final Regulations for the Amendments to the Individuals with Disabilities Education Act, P.L. 105-17 (1997)*

"In order to ensure that students with disabilities are fully included in the accountability benefits of State and district-wide assessments, it is important that the State include results for children with disabilities whenever the State reports results for other children. When a State reports data about State or district-wide assessments at the district or school level for nondisabled children, it also must do the same for children with disabilities." (Reports Relating to Assessment, Discussion, p. 12565)

Box 7.5

— *Guidance on Standards, Assessments, and Accountability That Supplements the Elementary & Secondary Education Act as Amended by the Improving America's Schools Act of 1994, P.L. 103-382 (1997)*

"Focusing an accountability system on schools is driven by the belief that as long as schools understand their responsibility to serve every child and expect every child to learn, a strategy for improving schools can most effectively lift the achievement levels of all children." (V. Accountability and Improvements, p. 1 of 8)

— *Peer Reviewer Guidance for Evaluating Evidence of Final Assessments Under Title I of the Elementary & Secondary Education Act, P.L. 103-382 (1999)*

"Schools and districts know how well all of their students are doing in relation to a common set of State standards so that schools and districts can be held accountable and make improvements." (Part IA. Content, Grade Levels, and Administration, p. 6)

USING ASSESSMENT RESULTS ✖

It is not enough to report assessment data. The data must be used to improve student outcomes, and students with disabilities must be included in data-driven efforts to make improvements in the achievement levels of all students. Law and practice in most states require that in every district or school, parents, teachers, administrators, and community partners need to sit down together, look at the achievement data of all their children, and determine how to help all children succeed. This typically is called the "school improvement planning process," and most states provide a framework to help districts and schools use data-based decision making to make year-by-year progress in increasing achievement levels. These processes must include every child and must be focused on lifting the achievement levels of all children (see Box 7.5).

Box 7.6

━ *Peer Reviewer Guidance for Evaluating Evidence of Final Assessments Under Title I of the Elementary & Secondary Education Act, P.L. 103-382 (1999)*

"The law also permits LEAs to include other appropriate information in the profiles, such as data on teachers' qualifications; class size; and attendance, promotion rates and retention rates." (Part III. Reporting and Using Assessment Results in Accountability, pp. 50-51)

In law and in practice, these year-by-year incremental improvements in schooling are measured in an effort to look at "adequate yearly progress" toward state- and district-set achievement goals. Most states have several measures of adequate yearly progress that include an emphasis on student achievement data but also may include other factors, such as teachers' qualifications, class size, attendance, promotion rates, and retention rates (see Box 7.6).

It is in the reporting of data, the public accountability for all students' success, and the process of improving schooling where the full benefit of inclusion in assessment comes to fruition. In the U.S. educational system, we truly treasure what we measure, and we measure what we treasure.

✖ CONTINUOUS IMPROVEMENT AT THE SCHOOL LEVEL

Many states have well-defined continuous-improvement models for districts and schools to use, and there are a number of organizations that provide models for adoption in districts and schools. Almost all of these models show a straightforward cycle of analyzing data, planning, implementing change policies, and monitoring results (see Figure 7.1).

The idea of local school staff and their parent and community partners sitting down to identify needs and plan ways to help all students be successful is very powerful, but many school improvement teams find the process to be challenging. And many district and school improvement teams do not understand that all students, including those with disabilities, are to benefit from the school improvement process.

The following example shows a story of one small school district that developed skills at truly inclusive school improvement planning. You'll see how the planning process relied on the willingness of the planning team to ask good questions and look for creative solutions rather than just on "looking at the numbers."

Inclusive School Improvement Planning at Cedar Creek

Cedar Creek School District is a rural, small school district that draws students from five small towns, one Indian reservation, and a large farming community. Over 14% of its students have disabilities; there is a large Title I–eligible group of students; and there is 12% minority enrollment, primarily Native American children, Hispanic children whose families were formerly migrant

Figure 7.1. Continuous Improvement Model

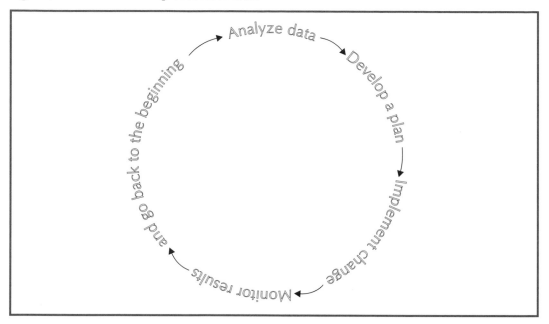

workers, and a small population of recent immigrants. For over 20 years, the school board has consistently and publicly supported the belief that all of their students can be successful, and they have provided consistent leadership and support so that their teachers can be successful in their efforts at giving every student the opportunities they need. When the state began working to define content and performance standards, the district volunteered to become a pilot partner in the effort. The superintendent and school board told the community that they saw the shift to standards as an opportunity to clearly define what "success" meant for all of their students.

The district had a comprehensive testing program supplemented by additional instructional and curricular data-gathering methods, and the district relied heavily on teacher teams to identify areas of strength and weakness in instruction and curriculum and to design staff development to address issues. When the standards-based state assessments were implemented, the schools looked forward to additional information about their students.

But when the reports of student results from the new standards-based assessments were studied, the planning team was puzzled. They were concerned that some students were not at the proficient levels, but the overall summary of student performance didn't tell them enough about whether there were patterns in how students were doing. They were able to look at results by variables such as disability status, ethnicity, and free- and reduced-lunch groupings, but those numbers did not show any clear patterns from which they could develop an instructional improvement plan.

As the planning team members continued to think and reflect on what they saw, they asked the principals what other data would help them understand how all of their students were doing. One of the principals suggested that they dig a little deeper into the data, and with the help of one of the computer teachers, they developed their own database and were able to look at the student results in many different ways.

They also added data that they collected locally. They found that different minority groups were performing differently at different grade levels. For example, Native American students were performing well at elementary school level, but showed a startling drop in performance at the junior high level. This finding prompted some analysis of school culture across the district. As a result, they developed a plan for restructuring the junior high school to foster a greater sense of community and mutual support at that age level.

Then, they found that students with learning disabilities and cognitive disabilities were achieving at rates that exceeded expectations but that students with emotional or behavioral disabilities were not. Again, the planning team decided to look for more information. They asked staff and parents of these students to work with them to identify what was working and what was not. They found that there were high rates of disciplinary problems that were interfering with learning, and they concluded that although the staff had received good training on methods to ensure that students with learning disabilities are successful in general education classrooms, they had not addressed positive behavioral supports for the staff *and* for parents. That became an additional part of their staff development plan.

The most surprising discovery made by this tenacious planning group was that when all of the factors contributing to student success were teased out and analyzed, one factor seemed to contribute most powerfully to whether students were successful or not: attendance. Regardless of minority status, disability status, or economic status, if a student missed more than 9 days of school per semester, his or her achievement levels were lowered. There appeared to be a correlation between some categories of students and a tendency for absenteeism, and these at-risk groups did include students with disabilities.

The planning team suggested to the school board that some ad hoc committees of students, community members, leaders from some of the affected minority communities, and staff begin discussions about how the attendance challenges could be addressed. The planning team also encouraged the school board to continue an experimental "school within a school" project-based learning option in the high school, because there appeared to be better attendance rates for at-risk students there, based on the first 2 years of that option. And in that school-within-a-school option, there were students with a full range of abilities and skills—including students with the most significant disabilities—and there was early evidence to show that *all* of these students were experiencing success.

We hope that the picture of what the school improvement planning process looks like at Cedar Creek helps you understand that the use of data to improve schooling for all students is as much art as science. Committed, concerned community and school partners are more critical to the success of improvement planning than are all the data any of us could possibly generate. But by having high-quality data reflecting the progress and needs of *all* students, thoughtful planning teams have a better chance of ensuring that all students can be successful.

✖ AUDIENCES FOR THE INFORMATION

Having a thoughtful school improvement planning team is a critical component of the effective use of assessment reports. But the general public, news media, and other educators also need good information about what alternate-assessment scores mean. We need to ensure that these results are seen as legitimate and important if we hope to have meaningful change occur to benefit these students. This brings us back to the scoring dilemma we discussed earlier in this chapter: If almost all students in the alternate assessment receive "0" or "1" scores against an absolute standard, what does that suggest to outside observers? We can project a couple of different interpretations uninformed observers can make: First, they may see these students as a burden for schools, because almost nothing the school can do will improve those scores against the absolute standard; second, they will be reluctant to serve students with significant disabilities because of the effect on their school reports, and we may find increasing numbers of schools refusing to house certain types of programs and services. It may be that having performance levels that measure a relative standard, where a student can achieve a "4" score with hard work and support, may give more incentive for more and better services and may also tell us more about the quality of the school program. For example, if a school improvement team and the community learn that many of their students with significant disabilities received lower scores due to "inappropriateness" of the tasks, wouldn't that suggest some improvements that could be made? Alternatively, what if the scores for the alternate assessment participants were uniformly high and scoring documentation complimented the school for appropriate and high-quality skill levels of the students, along with evidence of generalizability of skills to multiple settings and increased independence? Wouldn't that be fit for a glowing headline in the local newspaper?

The danger of the relative standard for scoring and reporting of alternate assessment results is that we risk lowering expectations. The attitudes and beliefs in the inner circle of an IEP team about how high is high enough for expectations for these students are a key variable in controlling for this risk. It goes back to staff development, training, and support. The lessons about sustainable innovation reviewed in Chapter 6 are helpful as we think about how to ensure that every IEP team member for every student has a clear understanding of the value of high expectations.

How Lara's State Is Scoring, Reporting, and Using Alternate Assessment Results

Scoring Alternate Assessments in Lara's State

In Lara's state, the alternate assessment process she participated in last year was a pilot and was not implemented statewide. This year, her state is implementing alternate assessments statewide for the first time. One of the major issues the state is now faced with is, "What do we do with these alternate assessments once they are completed?" Their first discussions have been about the scoring process. They considered having teachers score the alternate assessments for their own students, but they realized that it is difficult to be objective when scoring the work of students they saw and worked with every day. They decided not to have a testing company score the assessments because of the important knowledge of students with significant disabilities that few scorers would have. Another consideration was to have a select group of teachers meet at a central location in the summer and score the assessments for the whole state. That seemed to be the best option, but another consideration was the importance of using actual alternate assessments as staff development tools. They realized that there could be no greater training tool than actual student work, viewed and rated by professional peers. Planning for scoring-training sessions is underway, and the sessions will begin in the summer of 2001.

Reporting Alternate Assessment Results in Lara's State

Once scoring is complete, Lara's state needs to report the results. In some states, a decision has been made to just score all alternate assessment participants at the lowest level or even one level below the lowest level. Lara's state, however, is determined to make the scores of alternate assessment participants, like Lara, count at the state level. They have developed some principles to guide their reporting practices and are now working out the logistics. A summary of the principles that will guide reporting practices in Lara's state follows:

- Data from all test takers will be included in performance reports.

- Accountability reports will include testing information on all students who participate in the state assessment, including alternate assessment participants.

- Rates of nonparticipation of students with disabilities and the reasons for the nonparticipation will be included in reports. Reporting the reason for nonparticipation will assist in pinpointing ways to increase participation of students with disabilities in assessments.

Communicating Alternate Assessment Results in Lara's State

Assessment personnel in Lara's state plan to communicate specifically about how students participate in assessments and give clear information about the level of performance of the students. Individual student reports will be distributed to schools and parents. These reports will show each student's performance levels. School-level results showing data for all assessment participants will be produced for schools and districts. A state report will display assessment data for all the districts and schools in the state. To protect the privacy of individual students, however, there will not be reports issued on schools with less than 10 alternate assessment participants.

Parents will be informed about the reporting policy for their child's data. Parents of students with disabilities will be made aware of how their children's scores will be used in the public reporting of results. Parents will be given notification as to how test scores for alternate assessment participants will be reported along with those of the majority of students.

Using Alternate Assessment Data in Lara's State

Lara's state has discussed several purposes for collecting data on the results of education. One purpose is to improve instruction. Public reporting will provide the citizens of Lara's state with information about how schools are doing and will serve as an accountability tool for education throughout the state. Statewide educational accountability reports on the condition of public education will include assessment results for school districts along with nontest performance measures and indicators believed to have a direct impact on student results (e.g., attendance rates, dropout rates).

How Did Alternate Assessment Data Help Lara?

This was the first year that Lara's parents and teachers realized that she could communicate and that she could work on increasing her communication skills. Her team realized, in hindsight, that Lara had been screaming to communicate in the past. For example, when something was being done to her and she screamed, the process stopped. Once they began seeing Lara's behavior more in the context of standards, they realized that she had been communicating all along, in her own way, but no one had seen screaming as communication. Now, they can work on modifying the screaming into other ways to communicate.

How Did Alternate Assessment Data Help Lara's Teachers?

Lara's teachers found that an important part of the whole process of alternate assessment has been the opportunity for teachers who work with students with significant and multiple disabilities to get together and learn from each other. Developing the assessments and scoring are activities that have been used to build a network of people who may not have had opportunities to work together in the past and to learn things from others that they may never have thought of on their own. For example, Lara's teachers found that she screamed when she heard music—so they stopped the music. They videotaped this process and showed it to another teacher who said, "I think she's singing!" Sure enough, Lara wasn't crying while she screamed, as she often did when in distress. Maybe she really was singing!

In addition to what Lara learned throughout the year was what was in all of this for her teachers. One of Lara's special education teachers summed it up by saying, "Last year, I felt like I was babysitting. Now, I feel like I am teaching. I am now a professional, and I have to do my job well, because I'll be held accountable!" Here are additional comments from Lara's team:

- "The biggest thing I see is now I know what I'm supposed to be doing, and I have an idea of where I need to head with each student."

- "Now I'm being held accountable for teaching—just like everyone else in the school."

- "It focused my instruction and what I need to pay attention to."

- "Now I'm teaching and not just babysitting."

- "It is powerful and kind of cool when you get to the end of the year and everyone is in the teachers' lounge whining about assessments—and now I can join them!"

- "I know I have to do my job well because my students are going to be counted, and I am accountable for what they have learned."

- "Now I have data to talk about; I don't just say, 'She looks better.' I have something quantifiable."

- "It's hard work including students who have never been part of the system. It took a lot of advocacy, which has really reenergized my work."

- "With data, I can actually show that something happened. I found a lot of times as a 'self-contained' teacher, I would say, 'My kids are doing so well,' and no one believed me."

8

Tying It All Together

A Progress Report on Lara

We heard recently from one of Lara's special education teachers. She wrote,

You should see Lara now! She has progressed so much! I know it looks like small increments to others, but for her, it is leaps and bounds. Just this week, we hooked her switch up to a tape player so that she can turn music on and off. It is so wonderful to see Lara begin to take control of her environment (even if I don't appreciate her choice in music—kids these days!). Lara is also in a general education class for weights and conditioning. Who would have thought that Lara could ever lift weights! Using what we now know about standards, we were able to work with the general education teacher, physical therapist, and special education teacher to design a program for Lara that gives her a workout, increases her fitness, and meets some part of the standards. Lara has gained 7 pounds and the doctor has commented that she has developed some muscles—he was impressed with what we are doing. When I walked into Lara's classroom one day this week, Lara saw me and immediately began waving her arm to activate a switch. The paraprofessional who was working with her said, "Oh, you want to show your teacher what you've learned today?" Lara screeched and kept that arm moving until she got a switch. It made me cry. Lara's mom came to school a couple weeks ago and cried through the whole class period, still rejoicing in the new realization that her daughter can do so much. Her parting comment was a hearty "thank you" to all of us for getting the team focused on the standards and on what Lara can do rather than what she can't do.

✖ IMPROVING ALTERNATE ASSESSMENTS

"So, how's it going there, then?" This is one of our favorite questions when we want to cut through a bunch of bureaucratic mumbo jumbo and find out how something is working, really. We have learned in our collective experience to always take the time to look back, especially after starting something new, figure out what we did, how we did, and most important, how we can do a better job in the future. Implementing alternate assessments is intense, especially at first, and especially as we make the shift toward high educational standards. While doing this type of intense work, it is hard, as they say, to see the forest for the trees.

In the district where one of the authors taught, the teachers take one evening after school each year, with comfortable clothes and lots of food, to evaluate what they have done and look toward the future. They have a facilitator and use a formal evaluation process—it consists primarily of brainstorming what worked and what didn't and then figuring out how to continue what worked and fix what didn't. They are open and honest and creative and have made many wonderful improvements for students. As you evaluate your alternate assessment system, some of the questions you might ask, based on the information covered in this book, are presented in Figure 8.1.

This kind of systematic questioning, especially done by the people most affected by the alternate assessment at the local level, can lead to improvement of your alternate assessment year by year. Collegial action research tools, such as the staff evaluation and planning session described earlier, can make the difference between alternate assessments that benefit families, students, and educators and official "compliance" assessments. Just as the data from alternate assessments must be used in school improvement processes to benefit students, so too must we use the knowledge and insight of the practitioners to improve alternate assessment processes! But the time spent on improving the alternate assessment is worth it, because there are potential benefits for students, parents, teachers, and systems.

✖ THINKING IT THROUGH: WHO BENEFITS FROM ALTERNATE ASSESSMENTS?

What are the benefits of alternate assessments for students, parents, teachers, and systems? How will we each answer the question, "What's in it for us?" We'll turn here to comments we've heard from teachers and other team members from states that have been using alternate assessment for at least a year. Here's a sample of what they said:

- Teachers of students with significant disabilities see themselves as professionals—not babysitters—once they realize that their students can reach much higher expectations than in the past. Standards are good for kids!

Figure 8.1. Improving Alternate Assessments: Key Questions for Each Step of the Process

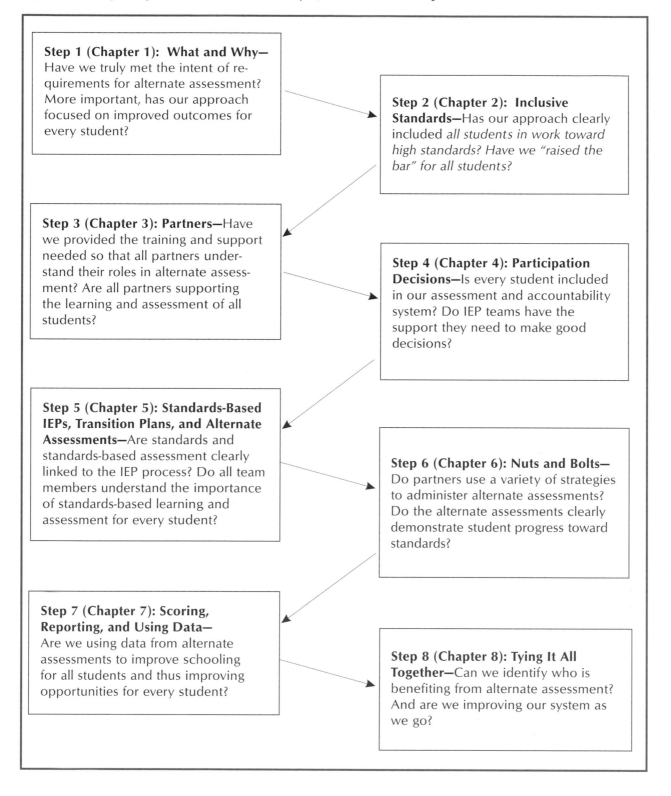

Step 1 (Chapter 1): What and Why— Have we truly met the intent of requirements for alternate assessment? More important, has our approach focused on improved outcomes for every student?

Step 2 (Chapter 2): Inclusive Standards—Has our approach clearly included *all students in work toward high standards? Have we "raised the bar"* for all students?

Step 3 (Chapter 3): Partners—Have we provided the training and support needed so that all partners understand their roles in alternate assessment? Are all partners supporting the learning and assessment of all students?

Step 4 (Chapter 4): Participation Decisions—Is every student included in our assessment and accountability system? Do IEP teams have the support they need to make good decisions?

Step 5 (Chapter 5): Standards-Based IEPs, Transition Plans, and Alternate Assessments—Are standards and standards-based assessment clearly linked to the IEP process? Do all team members understand the importance of standards-based learning and assessment for every student?

Step 6 (Chapter 6): Nuts and Bolts— Do partners use a variety of strategies to administer alternate assessments? Do the alternate assessments clearly demonstrate student progress toward standards?

Step 7 (Chapter 7): Scoring, Reporting, and Using Data— Are we using data from alternate assessments to improve schooling for all students and thus improving opportunities for every student?

Step 8 (Chapter 8): Tying It All Together—Can we identify who is benefiting from alternate assessment? And are we improving our system as we go?

- I think, in our school, for the first time, these students are seen as who they really are, individuals with a unique personality. This happened as soon as more of the staff and community became involved with them through standards-based instruction and alternate assessment!
- Standards and alternate assessments bring together the best skills of both general and special educators.
- Alignment between instruction and assessment is increased with alternate assessment.
- Alternate assessment ensures that students are represented in the school accountability system and that's important to getting noticed on our improvement committee.
- Students have multiple ways to show what they know and can do.
- This really gives us a look at how things are going—and it forces accountability for what happens in the classroom.
- The structure of alternate assessments helps teachers organize instruction and do better individual student planning, and it also gives us good systems information.
- Parents really love the collections of student work. It showcases a student's performance and helps us all see the growth that's really happening.
- The need for ongoing assessment of IEP goals is revitalized. That's a skill that had been lost in many special education classrooms.

The last comment is worth thinking about. It is so easy to slide into the situation where we say, "I don't assess kids—it takes too much time away from teaching." From there, we soon find ourselves having lesson plans that are the same from year to year—with units taught for specific periods of time each semester. Each unit might have a specific list of IEP goals for each participating student. For example, if the student is scheduled into a home-living class, he or she has an IEP goal addressing cooking or cleaning. Soon, we find ourselves in the situation where nothing is individualized, and assessment really is a waste of time because nothing changes as a result of the assessments.

Alternate assessment requirements have helped many special educators remember that the only way to individualize instruction is to continually assess the progress of each student. There are many ways to do this: Use charts, videotapes, daily logs, weekly goal sheets, and student contracts that are reviewed on a regular basis. Some of the record-keeping processes are too time consuming and add less than they take away from a student's instruction. These can be quickly discarded in favor of techniques that are more efficient and informative. All of the information can be shared with parents at team meetings and used to develop very individualized plans. Assessment information is easily compiled for alternate assessments. That's a *huge* benefit of alternate assessment when it occurs!

Many of the benefits of alternate assessments will emerge slowly, as parents, students, teachers, and other team members build their skills in standards-based planning. One of the authors has a story she thinks relates to that process:

I remember when my mom taught me to bake bread. She gave me careful instructions, along with a detailed written recipe, and then watched as I fumbled through each step. The next time I baked bread, I did it on my own. I took a beautiful loaf out of the oven and served it to my family at dinner. Well, the loaf looked great, but I had forgotten to add the salt and ended up tossing the whole thing out to the squirrels in the back yard. The next time I baked bread, I remembered the salt and forgot the yeast—even the squirrels didn't eat that loaf! I finally got it right and have had perfect loaves most of the time since! Building standards-based IEPs reminds me of my bread-baking experience. It takes a careful process that can be written down and taught, but it takes practice to get right. Any step that is missed means a trip back to the drawing board.

We have given you instructions, even a detailed written "recipe," and we hope we have guided you through each step. But for you and your students to benefit, you need to keep practicing! In the first chapter, we suggested that it is important to apply the information in the rest of the book to students *you* know and work with for *you* to get answers you can believe to our "tough questions." We asked you to choose a student you care about and work with us and that student through the remaining chapters. We said that at the end of the book, we would pose these questions again and, again, ask you to answer them for yourself.

So, we will ask those questions again and hope that you will find your answers. We'll review the answers we have come up with as well, chapter by chapter.

OUR ANSWERS TO THE TOUGH QUESTIONS ✖

Chapter 1

TOUGH QUESTIONS

Why should standards-based reform affect students who receive special education services, because their education plan is already individualized and tailored to their unique learning needs?

I understand why we need to measure student progress toward standards, and expect schools to help all students be successful. But students with the most severe disabilities can't really learn anything other than some really basic functional skills anyway, can they?

What difference does it make whether we are measuring students with the most severe disabilities? There really are not many of them anyway, and the gains they make are almost immeasurable.

OUR RESPONSE

The premise of standards-based reform is very different from the previous premise of a bell-shaped curve for student performance. The premise is that all students can be expected to learn, although some may need more time and varied instruction, and that high expectations can be operationalized by articulating what all students must know and be able to do and to what levels. The challenge facing us is to provide opportunities for all students to learn and to hold schools accountable for their learning.

In practical terms, for school reform to benefit all students, we need to have a broad level of information about how all students are doing against common standards. Then we step back and ask several questions: What do our data tell us about our programs?

How are all students improving over time? How can we use this information to help us programmatically? Alternate assessments give us important information as we systematically look at how our students are doing against higher standards than have been held before. Knowing how they are doing will help us make a difference in designing instruction to help them move forward.

If we improve our schools by measuring the progress of our students, then who should be measured? To ensure that all students have opportunities to learn to high standards, *all* students must be measured. Not *all* students will be assessed exactly the same way, but *all* students will fit into a system of assessment aligned to the same standards. Yet individual students sometimes require particular approaches to assessment to show what they know and are able to do.

We have shown throughout this book that all students can learn and that the progress of each student can be measured through alternate assessments. Now, when someone says, "Why count those students—they can't learn anything anyway," we will have actual data that shows that they can learn and have a right to be counted in efforts to improve schooling through standards-based reform.

Chapter 2

TOUGH QUESTIONS

What are the state standards? I've never been expected to use them with my students.

How does the alternate assessment fit into district and state standards? Most of the students I serve will never be able to read or do math!

My students are learning functional skills. How does that relate to standards-based learning and subject area knowledge and skills?

OUR RESPONSE

Content and performance standards give us commonly defined goals, commonly accepted targets for what children should know and be able to do. It is clear in federal law that all students receiving federally funded services must be held to the challenging standards that apply to all students. But it is also clear that students will vary in their performance levels—some students will learn to higher levels than others, even when all students have an opportunity to learn to high levels.

Will the way we teach all these students vary? Yes! And will some students need alternate ways of showing us what they know and how they are able to do these things? Yes! And will students vary on the level to which they perform along the path to the highest standard? Yes! But all students will be working toward these same high standards. If students are not learning along the path to the standards, it is the learning plan that needs changing, *not* the standards.

The purpose of alternate assessments is to assess the progress of students with significant disabilities toward standards. Nearly all states have developed education standards for students to meet. Most of these standards have been designed with grade-level benchmarks. Many states have expanded their standards to include functional skills, thus including all students within the same set of standards. What we suggest here is that by keeping students in the same set of standards and adjusting performance indicators to appropriate levels, you encourage the highest possible expectations, challenging the students to the highest possible outcomes.

Chapter 3

TOUGH QUESTIONS

Are special education teachers responsible for the whole process of administering alternate assessments?

What happens if parents refuse to have their children participate in state assessments, including alternate assessments?

School psychologists administer most of our placement assessments. Do alternate assessments need to be administered by them, too?

Paraprofessionals are unable to attend IEP meetings in our district. Because they are heavily involved in the education of students with disabilities, can they still be involved in alternate assessments?

OUR RESPONSE

The implementation of alternate assessments needs to be carried out through a partnership of many people, just as the education of children with disabilities needs a variety of partners to be successful. Several of these partners are members of a student's IEP team, whereas others, like paraprofessionals, may assist in the assessment process in other ways. Although school psychologists can be of great help in identifying tasks and assessment strategies, often it is the people who work most closely with the student, like general and special education teachers, parents, paraprofessionals, and even peers, who are in the best position to gather data.

Many IEP team members lack information about state and district standards and assessments. IEP team meetings are good times to provide information to team members, including parents, but probably should not be the very first time anyone hears about standards and assessment requirements. Parents of students with disabilities need the same information as other parents, and they need to understand the benefits of participation for their own child. They need information about how their child will be prepared to participate in assessments, information about assessment accommodations, how assessments relate to life in the future, and other related concerns.

IEP teams are charged with making assessment participation decisions. The entire IEP team makes participation decisions using the state's criteria, so it cannot just be a parent choice. When an IEP team recommends certain services for a child and the parent does not agree, the parent can initiate due process proceedings.

It is true that good teaching is a demanding job, in special education and general education. If you are creating instruction around the standards, giving students opportunities to learn about the standards, then having them do work that demonstrates their mastery of the standards is not an additional responsibility—it *is* our responsibility. All of us are facing the same kind of challenges as we transform our work with students so that it is really based on standards. You may have to change what you do, just as general education is working to align their instruction to standards and assessment, but it is not in addition to what we are supposed to be doing. It *is* what we are supposed to be doing. We are all in the same boat together. We need to collaborate and support one another as we all work at this important effort.

Chapter 4

TOUGH QUESTIONS

Who decides which students should participate in alternate assessments?

Should most students with disabilities participate in large-scale assessments?

Are some students too low functioning to participate in alternate assessments?

I have a student who does very poorly on state tests even though I think he can read most of the questions. He hardly ever finishes and has a hard time finding the right place to fill in the bubbles on the answer sheet. Should he participate in alternate assessments?

OUR RESPONSE

Participation decisions are made by a student's IEP team and documented on the IEP. Strategies for making effective participation decisions were covered in Chapter 4, but no matter how good the decision, if the right people do not know about it and it is not documented in a place where people know it can be found, new decisions may be made in a hurry for the wrong reasons by the wrong people.

The decision to participate in alternate assessments is *not* based on placement or disability category; it is based on a student's ability to participate in state assessments. Not all students in self-contained programs will participate in alternate assessments; and not all students in general education classes will participate in general assessments. Do not make decisions based on disability category or placement.

There are no exemptions for students receiving educational services. Students are to participate in general assessments with no accommodations or with accommodations, or they are to participate in the alternate assessment. Low expectations paired with poor test-taking skills, ineffective use of accommodations, and a fear that poor test takers will pull down school performance averages are reasons some students are placed in alternate assessments. With higher expectations, authentic instruction, increased test-taking skills, use of accommodations, and incentives for greater assessment participation, more students could participate in general assessments.

Chapter 5

TOUGH QUESTIONS

Do students with "maintenance only" IEPs need to address standards?

How will alternate assessments be correlated with the IEP?

What do we do if our state's IEP form does not mention standards or alternate assessments?

Is it possible to address standards and transition on the same IEP?

OUR RESPONSE

IEPs developed with standards in mind can offer students a broader range of educational opportunities than they have ever had before. Standards-based IEPs can also provide the information needed to complete alternate assessments. To give alternate assessment participants an opportunity to work toward standards, even at the most basic or functional levels, standards must be addressed on their IEPs.

Alternate assessment at its best is both an instructional and an assessment tool. You may want to review each student's IEP and look for opportunities to link ongoing instruction and assessment to alternate assessment data requirements—that is, identify what the student is already doing in a variety of settings that can be used to demonstrate progress toward standards. Measuring progress toward standards-based IEP goals and objectives and measuring progress toward standards for the alternate assessment can be one and the same.

IEP forms vary across the country and, within some states, even across districts. Standards may be addressed within the IEP, as an add-on, or not at all. It is important that IEP teams have a process that drives their planning and decision making and not be driven by items in the order that they appear on the form. IEP meetings that simply engage people in checking boxes on a streamlined compliance document may not result in plans that truly enable students to work toward standards or allow teams to make good decisions about participation in alternate assessments. Our best advice is to use the forms to fit the plan—don't try to develop a plan so that it will fit a rigid, compliance-oriented IEP form.

Last, all students need skills for success in today's world. How better to achieve that success than to have a good plan for the future, a future based on high standards? Transition planning, working toward high standards, and special education services are all about achieving success as an adult in today's world.

Chapter 6

TOUGH QUESTIONS

Most of my students don't complete pencil-and-paper assignments. How can I show what they're learning?

Who can collect data for an alternate assessment? What about parents, general education teachers, related-services people—is that appropriate?

Exactly what is a "body of evidence" for my students? Give me specific examples of what kinds of data are appropriate.

OUR RESPONSE

It is important to remember that *all* students can benefit from a variety of instruction and assessment strategies in daily classroom work. These assessments capture data that help us get a good picture of how every student is progressing toward standards. The use of a variety of assessment strategies, linked to instruction, can help us observe and monitor subtle or complex progress toward standards. For example, a variety of assessment strategies can help determine what learning is occurring for a student with the most challenging multiple disabilities where progress is slow and subtle. The strategies reviewed in Chapter 6 included observations, recollection (through interviews, surveys, or rating scales), and record review.

In Chapter 3, we discussed the roles of partners in instruction and assessment. The support of parents, general education teachers, related services personnel, and others are essential for all students with significant challenges to their learning. And these same partners are the keys to gathering rich data on how each student's learning is progressing. By using multiple strategies to collect data as well as multiple observers, you ensure that the data you collect into a body of evidence for each student will reflect true progress toward the standards.

Chapter 7

TOUGH QUESTIONS

Isn't special education only responsible for improvement of schooling for students with disabilities? Why would we want to be involved in our school's improvement processes for general education?

How can scores from alternate assessments fairly reflect both student progress against a standard and student progress against individualized student needs and abilities? Wouldn't all students participating in alternate assessment automatically score at the lowest level in state reporting systems?

What do the results from alternate assessment mean?

OUR RESPONSE

Special education has a responsibility to ensure that all students with IEPs have access to the general education curriculum and get the services they need to be successful. There is one system of general education, and to succeed in that system students who receive special education services must be part of the assessment and improvement processes for that system. There is a saying that we treasure what we measure or, alternatively, we measure what we treasure. If we throw away data for some of our students, we also risk throwing away opportunities for those students. As a bottom line, including students with disabilities in assessment and accountability systems ensures that they will be included in budgetary systems as well.

Under federal law and in practice in all states, all students are expected to work toward the same high expectations or standards. States and districts must measure how well students are doing by using assessments that are aligned to standards. Based on assessment results, school improvement teams work to improve curriculum and instruction so that all students can succeed. States, districts, and schools are accountable for the results of all children, and looking at the assessment results tells us whether schools are moving in the direction of success for all children.

There are concerns about how states and districts are scoring and reporting alternate assessment data. If we measure against an absolute standard of performance, many of the students who participate in the alternate assessment may not be able to show the gains they are in fact making. Yet we risk lowering expectations by selecting a relative standard of performance, which may give us more meaningful data. The attitudes and beliefs in the inner circle of an IEP team about how high is high enough for expectations for these students are key variables in controlling for this risk. It goes back to staff development, training, and support. The lessons about sustainable innovation reviewed in Chapter 6 are helpful as we think about how to ensure that every IEP team member for every student has a clear understanding of the value of high expectations.

AND WHY DO WE CARE? ⊠

- All children can learn.
- All children thrive in an atmosphere of high expectations about what they will learn.
- If all children are expected to learn and they have had opportunities to reach high expectations, all children can be successful.

Resource A
Legal References

TITLE I CITATIONS

Elementary & Secondary Education Act as Amended by the Improving America's Schools Act of 1994, P.L. 103-382 (1994). Web link: *http://www.ed.gov/legislation/ESEA/toc.html*

Guidance on Standards, Assessments, and Accountability That Supplements the Elementary & Secondary Education Act as Amended by the Improving America's Schools Act of 1994, P.L. 103-382 (1997). Web link: *http://www.ed.gov/offices/OESE/StandardsAssessment/*

Peer Reviewer Guidance for Evaluating Evidence of Final Assessments Under Title I of the Elementary & Secondary Education Act, P.L. 103-382 (1999). Web link: *http://www.ed.gov/offices/OESE/cpg.doc*

Letter and Attachment (Summary Guidance on the Inclusion Requirement for Title I Final Assessments) From Assistant Secretary for Elementary and Secondary Education Mike Cohen (April 6, 2000). Web link: *http://www.ed.gov/offices/OESE/saa/lessons.html* (additional guidance provided under) *http://www.ed.gov/offices/OESE/saa/update.html* from September 7, 2000)

IDEA CITATIONS

Amendments to the Individuals with Disabilities Education Act, P.L. 105-17 (1997). Web link: *http://www.ideapractices.org/law/IDEAMAIN.HTM*

Final Regulations for the Amendments to the Individuals with Disabilities Education Act, P.L. 105-17 (1999). Web link: *http://www.ideapractices.org/lawandregs.htm*

IDEA: Questions and Answers About Provisions in the Individuals with Disabilities Education Act Amendments of 1997 Related to Students with Disabilities and State and District-wide Assessments. Web link: *http://www.ed.gov/offices/OSERS/OSEP/OSEP memo0024Assessment.doc*

⊞ OFFICE OF CIVIL RIGHTS CITATIONS

The Use of Tests When Making High-Stakes Decisions for Students: A Resource Guide for Educators and Policymakers, U.S. Dept. of Education, Office of Civil Rights, July 6, 2000 Draft.

Resource B

Resources for Information and Assistance

■ **ASSOCIATIONS OF SERVICE PROVIDERS IMPLEMENTING IDEA REFORMS IN EDUCATION (ASPIIRE)**

The Council for Exceptional Children
1110 North Glebe Road
Arlington, VA 22201-5704
(877) CEC-IDEA
(703) 264-9480 TTY
Fax: (703) 264-1637
E-mail: ideapractices@cec.sped.org

Center for Research on Evaluation, Standards, and Student Testing (CRESST)
University of California, Los Angeles
Graduate School of Education and Information Studies
301 GSE & IS Building, Box 951522
300 Charles E. Young Drive North
Los Angeles, CA 90095-1522
(310) 206-1532
Fax: (310) 825-3883
Web site: http://cresst96.cse.ucla.edu

Education Commission of the States
707 17th Street, Ste 2700
Denver, CO 80202-3427
(303) 299-3600
Fax: 303-296-8332
E-mail: ecs@ecs.org

Elementary and Middle Schools Technical Assistance Center (EMSTAC)
American Institutes for Research
1000 Thomas Jefferson Street NW, Suite 400
Washington, DC 20007
(202) 944-5300
(877) 334-3499 TTY
Fax: (202) 944-5454
E-mail: emstac@air.org

ERIC Clearinghouse on Disabilities and Gifted Education
ERIC/OSEP Special Project
The Council for Exceptional Children
1110 North Glebe Road
Arlington, VA 22201-5704
(800) 328-0272 phone/TTY
E-mail: ericec@cec.sped.org

HEATH Resource Center
American Council on Education
One Dupont Circle NW, Suite 800
Washington, DC 20036-1193
(800) 544-3284 or (202) 939-9320 phone/TTY
(202) 833-5696 fax
E-mail: Heath@ace.nche.edu

IDEA Local Implementations by Local Administrators (ILIAD)
The Council for Exceptional Children
1110 North Glebe Road
Arlington, VA 22201-5704
(877) CEC-IDEA phone
(703) 264-9480 TTY
(703) 264-1627 fax
E-mail: ideapractices@cec.sped.org

National Association of State Directors of Special Education
1800 Diagonal Road, Ste 320
King Street Station I
Alexandria, VA 22314
(703) 519-3800
Fax: (703) 519-3808
Web Site: http://www.nasdse.org

National Center on Accessing the General Curriculum (NCAC)
Center for Applied Special Technology
39 Cross Street
Peabody, MA 01960
(978) 531-8555 phone
(978) 531-3110 TTY
(978) 531-0192 fax
E-mail: chitchcock@cast.org

National Center on Educational Outcomes (NCEO)
University of Minnesota
350 Elliott Hall
75 East River Road
Minneapolis, MN 55455
(612) 624-4073 phone
(612) 624-0879 fax
E-mail: scott027@tc.umn.edu

**National Center on Increasing the Effectiveness of State and Local
  Education Reform Efforts**
Consortium for Policy Research in Education (CPRE)
Graduate School of Education, University of Pennsylvania
3440 Market Street, Suite 560
Philadelphia, PA 19104-3325
(215) 573-0700
Fax: (215) 573-7914
Web site: http://www.upenn.edu/gse/cpre

National Center on Secondary Education and Transition (NCSET)
University of Minnesota
102 Pattee Hall
150 Pillsbury Drive SE
Minneapolis, MN 55455
(612) 624-2097 phone
(612) 624-9344 fax
E-mail: johns006@tc.umn.edu

National Center to Improve the Tools of Educators (NCITE)
College of Education
University of Oregon
805 Lincoln Street
Eugene, OR 97401
(541) 683-7543 phone
(541) 683-7543 fax
E-mail: jwallin@oregon.uoregon.edu

National Information Center for Children and Youth with Disabilities (NICHCY)
Academy for Educational Development
P.O. Box 1492
Washington, DC 20013-1492
(800) 695-0285 or (202) 884-8200 phone/TTY
(202) 884-8441 fax
E-mail: nichcy@aed.org

National Information Clearinghouse on Children Who Are Deaf-Blind (DB-LINK)
Western Oregon University
Teaching Research Division
345 North Monmouth Avenue
Monmouth, OR 97361
(800) 438-9376 phone
(800) 854-7013 TTY
(503) 838-8150 fax
E-mail: dblink@tr.wou.edu

National Transition Alliance for Youth with Disabilities (NTA)
Transition Research Institute
University of Illinois
113 Children's Research Center
51 Gerty Drive
Champaign, IL 61820
(217) 333-2325 phone/TTY
(217) 244-0851 fax
E-mail: leachlyn@uiuc.edu

Parents Engaged in Education Reform (PEER)
Federation for Children with Special Needs
1135 Tremont Street, Suite 420
Boston, MA 02120
(617) 236-7210 phone/TTY
(617) 572-2094 fax
E-mail: fcsninfo@fcsn.org

Policymaker Partnership (PMP) for Implementing IDEA '97
National Association of State Directors of Special Education
1800 Diagonal Road, Suite 320
Alexandria, VA 22314-2840
(877) IDEA-INFO or (703) 519-3800 phone
(703) 519-7008 TTY
(703) 519-3808 fax
E-mail: pmp@nasdse.org

Professional Development Leadership Academy: Enhancing Collaborative Partnerships for Systems Change

National Association of State Directors of Special Education
1800 Diagonal Road, Suite 320
Alexandria, VA 22314-2840
(703) 519-3800 x319 phone
(703) 519-7008 TTY
(703) 519-3808 fax
E-mail: karlm@nasdse.org

Technical Assistance for Parent Centers—the Alliance

PACER Center
8161 Normandale Boulevard
Bloomington, MN 55437
(888) 248-0822 or (952) 838-9000 phone
(952) 838-0190 TTY
(952) 838-0199 fax
E-mail: alliance@taalliance.org

Technical Assistance in Data Analysis, Evaluation, and Report Preparation

Westat
1650 Research Boulevard
Rockville, MD 20850
(301) 251-1500 phone
(301) 294-4475 fax
E-mail: Brauenm1@westat.com

⊞ REGIONAL RESOURCE AND FEDERAL CENTERS FOR SPECIAL EDUCATION

Federal Resource Center for Special Education (FRC)

Academy for Educational Development
1825 Connecticut Avenue NW
Washington, DC 20009
(202) 884-8215 phone
(202) 884-8200 TTY
(202) 884-8443 fax
E-mail: frc@aed.org

Northeast Regional Resource Center (NERRC)

Learning Innovations at WestEd
20 Winter Sport Lane
Williston, VT 05495
(802) 951-8226 phone
(802) 951-8213 TTY
(802) 951-8222 fax
E-mail: nerrc@aol.com
nerrc@wested.org

> *States served include Connecticut, Maine, Massachusetts, New Hampshire, New Jersey, New York, Rhode Island, and Vermont.*

Mid-South Regional Resource Center (MSRRC)

Human Development Institute
University of Kentucky
126 Mineral Industries Building
Lexington, KY 40506-0051
(859) 257-4921 phone
(859) 257-2903 TTY
(859) 257-4353 fax
E-mail: msrrc@ihdi.uky.edu

> *States served include Delaware, Kentucky, Maryland, North Carolina, South Carolina, Tennessee, Virginia, West Virginia, and the District of Columbia.*

Southeast Regional Resource Center (SERRC)

School of Education
Auburn University Montgomery
P.O. Box 244023
Montgomery, AL 36124-4023
(334) 244-3100 phone
(334) 244-3835 fax
E-mail: bbeale@edla.aum.edu

> *States served include Alabama, Arkansas, Florida, Georgia, Louisiana, Mississippi, Oklahoma, Puerto Rico, Texas, and the U.S. Virgin Islands.*

Great Lakes Area Regional Resource Center (GLARRC)

Center for Special Needs Populations
The Ohio State University
700 Ackerman Road, Suite 440
Columbus, OH 43202-1559
(614) 447-0844 phone
(614) 447-8776 TTY
(614) 447-9043 fax
E-mail: daniels.121@osu.edu

> *States served include Illinois, Indiana, Iowa, Michigan, Minnesota, Missouri, Ohio, Pennsylvania, and Wisconsin.*

Mountain Plains Regional Resource Center (MPRRC)

Utah State University

1780 North Research Parkway, Suite 112

Logan, UT 84341

(435) 752-0238 phone

(435) 753-9750 TTY

(435) 753-9750 fax

E-mail: cope@cc.usu.edu

> *States served include Arizona, Bureau of Indian Affairs (BIA), Colorado, Kansas, Montana, Nebraska, New Mexico, North Dakota, South Dakota, Utah, and Wyoming.*

Western Regional Resource Center (WRRC)

1268 University of Oregon

Eugene, OR 97403-1268

(541) 346-5641 phone

(541) 346-0367 TTY

(541) 346-5639 fax

E-mail: wrrc@oregon.uoregon.edu

> *States served include Alaska, American Samoa, California, Commonwealth of the Northern Mariana Islands, Federated States of Micronesia, Guam, Hawaii, Idaho, Nevada, Oregon, Republic of the Marshall Islands, Republic of Palau, and Washington.*

References

Custer, R. L., Schell, J., McAlister, B. D., Scott, J. L., & Hoepfl, M. (2000). *Using authentic assessment in vocational education* (Information Series No. 381). Columbus, OH: ERIC Clearinghouse on Adult, Career, and Vocational Education.

Education Commission of the States. (1999). *Education accountability systems in 50 states.* Denver, CO: Author.

Educators in Connecticut's Pomperaug Regional School District 15. (1996). *A teacher's guide to performance-based learning and assessment.* Middlebury, CT: Author.

Elliott, J., Ysseldyke, J. Thurlow, M., & Erickson, R. (1997). *Providing accommodations for students with disabilities in state and district assessments* (NCEO Policy Directions 7). Minneapolis: University of Minnesota, National Center on Educational Outcomes.

Erickson, K. A., & Koppenhaver, D. A. (1998, Fall). Using the "write talk-nology" with Patrik. *Teaching Exceptional Children,* 58-65.

Gersten, R., Chard, D., & Baker, S. (2000). Factors enhancing sustained use of research-based instructional practices. *Journal of Learning Disabilities, 33*(5), 445-457.

Giangreco, M. F., Cloninger, C. J., & Iverson, V. S. (1998). *Choosing outcomes and accommodations for children: A guide to educational planning for students with disabilities* (2nd ed.). Baltimore, MD: Brookes.

Giangreco, M. F., Dennis, R. E., Edelman, S. W., & Cloninger, C. J. (1994). Dressing your IEPs for the general education climate. *Remedial and Special Education, 15,* 288-296.

Hobbs, T., & Westling, D. L. (1998, Fall). Promoting successful inclusion through collaborative problem-solving. *Teaching Exceptional Children,* 12-19.

Kleinert, H. L., Kennedy, S., & Kearns, J. F. (1999). The impact of alternate assessments: A statewide teacher survey. *The Journal of Special Education, 32*(2), 93-102.

Koretz, D., Stecher, B., Klein, S., & McCaffrey, D. (1994). The Vermont Portfolio Assessment Program: Findings and implications. *Educational Measurement: Issues and Practice, 13*(3), 5-16.

Newmann, F. M., Secada, W. G., & Wehlage, G. G. (1995). *A guide to authentic instruction and assessment: Vision, standards and scoring.* Madison, WI: Center on Organization and Restructuring of Schools.

Northeast and Islands Regional Educational Laboratory at Brown University. (1999, March). Creating large-scale assessment portfolios that include English language learners. *Perspectives on Policy and Practice,* 1-4.

Quenemoen, R., & Quenemoen, A. (1999). School to adult life: Alma's story. In V. Gaylord, D. Johnson, & T. Wallace (Eds.), *Impact: Feature Issue on School-to-Work and Students with Disabilities.* Minneapolis: University of Minnesota, Institute on Community Integration.

Rogers, S., & Graham, S. (2000) *The high performance toolbox: Succeeding with performance tasks, projects, and assessments* (3rd ed.). Evergreen, CO: Peak Learning Systems.

Salvia, J., & Ysseldyke, J. E. (2001). *Assessment* (8th ed.). Boston: Houghton Mifflin.

Shepard, L. A. (2000). The role of assessment in a learning culture. *Educational Researcher, 29*(7), 4-14.

Siegel-Causey, E., McMorris, C., McGowen, S., & Sands-Buss, S. (1998, Fall). In junior high you take earth science: Including a student with severe disabilities into an academic class. *Teaching Exceptional Children,* 66-72.

Stiggins, R. J. (2000). *Student-involved classroom assessment* (3rd ed.). Upper Saddle River, NJ: Merrill Prentice Hall.

Taylor, C. S., & Nolen, S. B. (1996). What does the psychometrician's classroom look like? Reframing assessment concepts in the context of learning. *Education Policy Analysis Archives, 4*(17) [Online].

Thompson, S. J., & Thurlow, M. L. (2000). *State alternate assessments: Status as IDEA alternate assessment requirements take effect* (Synthesis Report 35). Minneapolis: University of Minnesota, National Center on Educational Outcomes. *http://www.coled.umn.edu/nceo*

Thurlow, M. L., Elliott, J. L., & Ysseldyke, J. E. (1998). *Testing students with disabilities: Practical strategies for complying with district and state requirements.* Thousand Oaks, CA: Corwin.

Wiggins, G., & McTigue, J. (1998). *Understanding by design.* Alexandria, VA: Association for Supervision and Curriculum Development.

Ysseldyke, J. E., & Olsen, K. R. (1997). *Putting alternate assessment into practice: What to measure and possible sources of data.* (Synthesis Report 28). Minneapolis, MN: University of Minnesota, National Center on Educational Outcomes. *http://www.coled.umn.edu/nceo*

Ysseldyke, J. E., Thurlow, M. L., McGrew, K. S., & Shriner, J. G. (1994). *Recommendations for making decisions about the participation of students with disabilities in statewide assessment programs* (Synthesis Report 15). Minneapolis: University of Minnesota, National Center on Educational Outcomes.

Recommended Reading

:: CHAPTER 1

Goldberg, M., Guy, B., & Moses, J. A. (1999). *Education reform: What does it mean for students with disabilities?* (NTN Parent Brief). Minneapolis: University of Minnesota, National Transition Network.

Heubert, J. P., & Hauser, R. M. (Eds.). (1999). *High stakes testing for tracking, promotion, and graduation.* Washington, DC: National Research Council.

Landau, J. K., Vohs, J. R., & Ramano, C. A. (1998). *All kids count: Including students with disabilities in statewide assessment programs* (PEER Project). Boston: Federation for Children with Special Needs.

McDonnell, L. M., McLaughlin, M. J., & Morison, P. (1997). *Educating one and all: Students with disabilities and standards-based reform.* Washington, DC: National Academy Press.

National Center on Educational Outcomes. (2000). *Alternate assessment forum 2000: Connecting into a whole.* Minneapolis: University of Minnesota, National Center on Educational Outcomes. *http://www.coled.umn.edu/nceo/OnlinePubs/Forum2000/ForumReport2000.htm*

Olsen, K. (1999, May). *What principles are driving development of state alternate assessments?* Lexington: University of Kentucky, Mid-South *Regional Resource Center.* *http://www.ihdi.uky.edu/msrrc/whatprincip.htm*

Olson, J. F., Bond, L., & Andrews, C. (1999). *Annual survey of state student assessment programs.* Washington, DC: Council of Chief State School Officers.

Thompson, S. J., & Thurlow, M. L. (1999). *1999 State special education outcomes: A report on state activities at the end of the century.* Minneapolis: University of Minnesota, National Center on Educational Outcomes. *http://www.coled.umn.edu/nceo*

Thompson, S. J., & Thurlow, M. L. (2000). *State alternate assessments: Status as IDEA alternate assessment requirements take effect* (Synthesis Report 35). Minneapolis:

University of Minnesota, National Center on Educational Outcomes. *http://www. coled. umn.edu/nceo*

✖ CHAPTER 2

American Federation of Teachers. (1999). *Making standards matter.* Washington, DC: Author.

Bauer, A. M., & Myree, G. (2001). *Adolescents and Inclusion: Transforming secondary schools.* Baltimore: Brookes.

Giangreco, M. F., Cloninger, C. J., & Iverson, V. S. (1998). *Choosing outcomes and accommodations for children: A guide to educational planning for students with disabilities* (2nd ed.). Baltimore: Brookes.

Gratz, D. B. (2000). High standards for whom? *Phi Delta Kappan, 81*(9), 681-687.

Kerzner, D., & Gartner, A. (1998). *Standards and inclusion—Can we have both?* (Video). Arlington, VA: Council for Exceptional Children.

McLaughlin, M. J., Nolet, V., Rhim, L. M., & Henderson, K. (1999). Integrating standards including all students. *Teaching Exceptional Children, 31*(3), 66-71.

National Association of State Boards of Education. (1999). *Reaching to the sky: Policy to support the achievement of students with disabilities.* Alexandria, VA: Author.

National Research Council. (1999). *Testing, teaching, and learning: A guide for states and school districts.* Washington, DC: National Academy Press.

Nolet, V., & McLaughlin, M. (2000). Accessing the general curriculum: Making schools work for students with disabilities. Thousand Oaks, CA: Corwin.

✖ CHAPTER 3

DeBoer, A., & Fister, K. (1995). *Working together: Tools for collaborative teaching.* Longmont, CO: Sopris West.

DeStefano, L., & Shriner, J. (2000, June). *The role of teacher decision making in participation and accommodation of students with disabilities in large-scale assessment.* Paper presented at the 30th Annual Council of Chief State School Officers National Conference on Large-Scale Assessment, Snowbird, UT.

Friend, M., & Cook, L. (1996). *Interactions: Collaboration skills for school professionals* (2nd ed.). White Plains, NY: Longman.

Pickett, M. L. (1996). *State of the art report on paraeducators in education and related services.* New York: City University of New York, National Resource Center for Paraeducators in Education and Related Services, Center for Advanced Study in Education.

Rainforth, B., & York-Barr, J. (1997). *Collaborative teams for students with severe disabilities* (2nd ed.). Baltimore: Brookes.

✖ CHAPTER 4

Burns, E. (1998). *Test accommodations for students with disabilities.* Springfield, IL: Charles C Thomas.

Elliott, J. L., Thurlow, M. L., & Ysseldyke, J. E. (1996). *Assessment guidelines that maximize the participation of students with disabilities in large-scale assessments: Characteristics and considerations* (Synthesis Report 25). Minneapolis: University of Minnesota, National Center on Educational Outcomes.

Elliott, S. N., Kratochwill, T. R., & Schulte, A. G. (1998). The assessment accommodation checklist: Who, what, where, when, why and how? *Teaching Exceptional Children, 31*(2), 10-14.

Fuchs, L. S., Fuchs, D., Eaton, S. B., Hamlett, C., & Karns, K. (2000). Supplementing teacher judgments of test accommodations with objective data sources. *School Psychology Review, 29*(1), 65-85.

Thurlow, M., Elliott, J., & Ysseldyke, J. (1997). *Testing students with disabilities: Practical strategies for complying with district and state requirements.* Thousand Oaks, CA: Corwin.

Thurlow, M. L., House, A., Boys, C., Scott, D., & Ysseldyke, J. (2000). *State participation and accommodations policies for students with disabilities: 1999 update* (Synthesis Report 33). Minneapolis: University of Minnesota, National Center on Educational Outcomes.

Thurlow, M. L., McGrew, K. S., Tindal, G., Thompson, S. J., Ysseldyke, J. E., & Elliott, J. L. (2000). *Assessment accommodations research: Considerations for design and analysis* (Technical Report 26). Minneapolis: University of Minnesota, National Center on Educational Outcomes.

Thurlow, M. L., Ysseldyke, J. E., & Silverstein, B. (1995). Testing accommodations for students with disabilities. *Remedial and Special Education, 16*(5), 260-270.

Tindal, G., & Fuchs, L. (1999). *A summary of research on test changes: An empirical basis for defining accommodations.* Lexington: University of Kentucky, Mid-South Regional Resource Center.

Tindal, G., Heath, B., Hollenbeck, K., Almond, P., & Harniss, M. (1998). Accommodating students with disabilities on large-scale tests: An experimental study. *Exceptional Children, 64*(4), 439-450.

Warlick, K., & Olsen, K. (1998, December). *Who takes the alternate assessment? State criteria.* Lexington: University of Kentucky, Mid-South Regional Resource Center. *http://www.ihdi.uky.edu/msrrc/whotakes.htm*

Resources on "Hot Button" Participation Issues

Almond, P., Quenemoen, R., Olsen, K., & Thurlow, M. (2000). *Gray areas of assessment systems* (Synthesis Report 32). Minneapolis: University of Minnesota, National Center on Educational Outcomes.

National Center on Educational Outcomes. (1999). *Forum on alternate assessment and "gray area" assessment.* Minneapolis: University of Minnesota, National Center on Educational Outcomes.

National Center on Educational Outcomes. (2000). *Alternate assessment forum 2000: Connecting into a whole.* Minneapolis: University of Minnesota, National Center on Educational Outcomes. *http://www.coled.umn.edu/nceo/OnlinePubs/forum2000/ForumReport2000.htm*

Thurlow, M. L., Elliott, J. L., & Ysseldyke, J. E. (1999). *Out-of-level testing: Pros and cons* (Policy Directions 9). Minneapolis: University of Minnesota, National Center on Educational Outcomes.

Thurlow, M. L., & Weiner, D. (2000). *Non-approved accommodations: Recommendations for use and reporting* (Policy Directions 11). Minneapolis: University of Minnesota, National Center on Educational Outcomes.

✖ CHAPTER 5

Algozzine, B., Ysseldyke, J., & Elliott, J. (1997). *Strategies and tactics for effective instruction* (2nd ed.). Longmont, CO: Sopris West.

Cheney, C. O. (2000). Ensuring IEP accountability in inclusive settings. *Intervention in School & Clinic, 35,* 185-190.

Elliott, J. L., & Thurlow, M. L. (2000). *Improving test performance of students with disabilities.* Thousand Oaks, CA: Corwin.

Hock, M. (2000). Ten reasons why we should use standards in IEPS. *In CASE, 42*(1), 5-7.

Office of Special Education and Rehabilitative Services. (2000). *A guide to the individualized education program.* Washington, DC: National Information Center for Children and Youth with Disabilities.

Shriner, J. G., Kim, D., Thurlow, M. L., & Ysseldyke, J. E. (1993). *IEPs and standards: What they say for students with disabilities* (Technical Report 5). Minneapolis: National Center on Educational Outcomes.

Ysseldyke, J. E., Algozzine, B., & Thurlow, M. L. (2000). *Critical issues in special education* (3rd ed.). Boston: Houghton Mifflin.

Resources on Transition Planning

American Federation of Teachers. (1999). *Reaching the next step: How school to career can help students reach high academic standards and prepare for good jobs.* Washington, DC: Author.

Center for Law and Education. (1999). *Ensuring access, equity, and quality for students with disabilities in school-to-work systems.* Minneapolis: University of Minnesota, National Transition Network.

Council for Exceptional Children. (1999). Student-centered transition programs critical for post-school success. *Today, 6*(3), 1-15.

Phelps, L. A., & Hanley-Maxwell, C. (1997). School-to-work transitions for youth with disabilities: A review of outcomes and practices. *Review of Educational Research, 67*(2), 197-226.

Rusch, F. R., & Chadsey, J. (Ed.). (1998). *Beyond high school: Transition from school to work.* Belmont, CA: Wadsworth.

Wehman, P. (2001). *Life beyond the classroom: Transition strategies for young people with disabilities* (3rd ed.). Baltimore: Brookes.

CHAPTER 6 ✖

Kearns, J. F., Kleinert, H. L., & Clayton, J. (1998). Principal supports for inclusive assessment: A Kentucky story. *Teaching Exceptional Children, 31*(2), 16-23.

Kleinert, H. L., Kearns, J. F., & Kennedy, S. (1997). Accountability for all students: Kentucky's alternate portfolio assessment for students with moderate and severe cognitive disabilities. *The Journal of the Association for Persons with Severe Handicaps, 22*, 88-101.

Olsen, K. (1999, May). *Alternate assessment issues and practices.* Lexington: University of Kentucky, Mid-South Regional Resource Center. *http://www.ihdi.uky.edu/msrrc/ aaissues.htm*

Warlick, K., & Olsen, K. (1999, April). *How to conduct alternate assessments: Practices in nine states.* Lexington: University of Kentucky, Mid-South Regional Resource Center. *http://www.ihdi.uky.edu/msrrc/howaa.htm*

CHAPTER 7 ✖

Bielinski, J., & Ysseldyke, J. (2000). *Interpreting trends in the performance of special education students* (Technical Report 27). Minneapolis: University of Minnesota, National Center on Educational Outcomes.

Erickson, R., Ysseldyke, J., & Thurlow, M. (1996). *Neglected numerators, drifting denominators, and fractured fractions: Determining participation rates for students with disabilities in statewide assessment programs* (Synthesis Report 23). Minneapolis: University of Minnesota, National Center on Educational Outcomes.

Stiggins, R. J. (2000). *Student-involved classroom assessment* (3rd ed.). Upper Saddle River, NJ: Merrill Prentice Hall.

Thurlow, M. L., House, A., Boys, C., Scott, D., & Ysseldyke, J. (2000). *State participation and accommodations policies for students with disabilities: 1999 update* (Synthesis Report 33). Minneapolis: University of Minnesota, National Center on Educational Outcomes.

Thurlow, M. L., Nelson, J. R., Teelucksingh, E., & Ysseldyke, J. E. (2000). *Where's Waldo? A third search for students with disabilities in state accountability reports* (Technical Report 25). Minneapolis: University of Minnesota, National Center on Educational Outcomes.

Ysseldyke, J. E., & Nelson, J. R. (1998). *Enhancing communication: Desirable characteristics for state and school district educational accountability reports* (Synthesis Report 30). Minneapolis: University of Minnesota, National Center on Educational Outcomes.

Ysseldyke, J. E., & Olsen, K. R. (1997). *Putting alternate assessments into practice: What to measure and possible sources of data* (Synthesis Report 28). Minneapolis: University of Minnesota, National Center on Educational Outcomes.

Ysseldyke, J. E., Thurlow, J. L., Erickson, R., Haigh, J., Moody, M., Trimble, S., & Insko, B. (1997). *Reporting school performance in the Maryland and Kentucky accountability systems: What scores mean and how they are used* (Maryland/Kentucky Report 2). Minneapolis: University of Minnesota, National Center on Educational Outcomes.

Ysseldyke, J. E., Thurlow, M. L., Langenfeld, K., Nelson, J. R., Teelucksingh, E., & Seyfarth, A. (1998). *Educational results for students with disabilities: What do the data tell us?* (Technical Report 23). Minneapolis: University of Minnesota, National Center on Educational Outcomes.

✛ CHAPTER 8

Kleinert, H. L., Kennedy, S., & Kearns, J. F. (1999). The impact of alternate assessments: A statewide teacher survey. *The Journal of Special Education, 32*(2), 93-102.

Langenfeld, K. L., Thurlow, M. L., & Scott, D. L. (1996). *High stakes testing for students: Unanswered questions and implications for students with disabilities* (Synthesis Report 26). Minneapolis: University of Minnesota, Institute on Community Integration.

Thurlow, M. L., Elliott, J. L., Ysseldyke, J. E., & Erickson, R. H. (1996). *Questions and answers: Tough questions about accountability systems and students with disabilities* (Synthesis Report 24). Minneapolis: University of Minnesota, Institute on Community Integration.

Index